WIDENING
the CIRCLE

Experiments in Christian Discipleship

"In an era when the cat's got the tongue of the American church, Shenk collects stories of communities experimenting with the most combustible force on earth: Christian prophetic imagination."
—*Rose Marie Berger, associate editor,* Sojourners *magazine*

"*Widening the Circle* is timely as the Mennonite tradition gathers interest and support among young people who are walking away from churches in a search for cultural engagement, authentic relationships, and a fresh focus on the teaching and ministry of Jesus."
—*Eddie Gibbs, Senior Professor, School of Intercultural Studies, Fuller Seminary*

"Joanna Shenk has sat with the faithful as they testify to the kingdom of God in our midst. These stories are relevant for all who desire to take Jesus seriously. After reading them, one is left with hope and inspiration for the journey."
—*Lucas Johnson, Baptist pastor and leader in the International Fellowship of Reconciliation*

"Anabaptism comes alive in these essays, in stories that bear witness to the movement of the Spirit in strange and familiar places. Joanna Shenk has assembled a book that invites us to become a home for those who are tired of destructive forms of Christianity."
—*Isaac S. Villegas, Pastor, Chapel Hill Mennonite Fellowship*

WIDENING
the CIRCLE

Experiments in Christian Discipleship

Edited by Joanna Shenk

Herald Press

Library of Congress Cataloging-in-Publication Data
Widening the circle : experiments in Christian discipleship / edited by Joanna
Shenk.
    p. cm.
  Includes bibliographical references.
  ISBN 978-0-8361-9558-3 (pbk.)
  1. Mennonites—History. 2. Anabaptists—History. 3. Church work—Men-
nonites. 4. Church work—Anabaptists. 5. Discipling (Christianity) 6. Men-
nonites—North America. 7. Anabaptists—North America. I. Shenk, Joanna.
II. Title: Experiments in Christian discipleship.
  BX8119.N66W53 2011
  289.709'045—dc23

                                                              2011036253

Unless otherwise noted, Scripture text is quoted, with permission, from the
New Revised Standard Version, © 1989, Division of Christian Education of
the National Council of Churches of Christ in the United States of America.

WIDENING THE CIRCLE
Copyright © 2011 by Herald Press, Harrisonburg, Virginia 22802
      Released simultaneously in Canada by Herald Press,
      Waterloo, Ontario N2L 6H7. All rights reserved.
Library of Congress Control Number: 2011036253
International Standard Book Number: 978-0-8361-9558-3
Printed in United States of America
Cover design by Jordan Kauffman

15 14 13 12 11   10 9 8 7 6 5 4 3 2 1

To order or request information, please call 1-800-245-7894 in the U.S. or
1-800-631-6535 in Canada. Or visit www.heraldpress.com.

To my family of origin—Jonny, Andy, Bekah, Nathan, Deborah, Alice, and Phil—and to my Elkhart community family.

Thank you for being on the spiral journey with me.

TABLE OF CONTENTS

Third Wave (1990s *to* Present)

FOREWORD

by Mary Jo Leddy and Ervin Stutzman

Listen in as Mary Jo Leddy, a Canadian Catholic activist and writer, and Ervin Stutzman, a leader in Mennonite Church USA, discuss the significance of Widening the Circle *for followers of Jesus—both within the Anabaptist tradition and far beyond it.*

Mary Jo: Reading this book is like seeing the ripples widen after a stone of great consequence has been cast into the waters of history. The Anabaptist story is not a big stone. It is small but weighty and consequential.

Ervin: On one level, this book is about Christian community. But on a deeper level, it is about much more. It is about the search for a deeper and more widely shared commitment to God's peace and justice in the world. It is about the ways that intentional communities develop and undergird a commitment to God's ways in an upside-down world.

Mary Jo: I am always in awe of the crucial Anabaptist insight into the ways of Empire. It is an insight forged in great suffering, and even though later generations may have become more comfortable and secure in their faith, they have carried the "dangerous memory"[1] of those who refused to bend to the will of emperors—whether political or religious.

I believe that this is the crucial gift that the Anabaptist tradition has to bring to all Christian efforts to live and act and believe as communities of faith. To quote the introduction of this book, "The great word of the Anabaptists was not 'faith' as it was for the reformers, but 'following.'" The counter-cultural "following" that is the Anabaptist way is all too easy to take for granted. However, it is as remarkable as it is authentic.

Ervin: When my wife Bonnie and I were married in 1974, we were drawn to the idea of Christian community. We joined a Mennonite voluntary service household and then expanded it a year later to include other Christians. We were drawn to the vision popularized by Dave and Neta Jackson's book *Living Together in a World Falling Apart.* We called our community the "Peace House" and wrote a covenant of commitment.

It was a great introduction to living together with people of different values and different needs. I look back with fondness and appreciation on those five years, when I learned a lot about myself as well as others. I learned that if I cannot change the people who sit at my table each day, I am not likely to change others beyond that circle.

Discipleship communities focus on the call to follow Jesus. They find ways to extend these commitments to everyday life, including difficult social problems. As the stories in this volume show, living together is not easy, particularly where members share their possessions with each other. The intensity of communal living can nurture people at their very core, but they can also exact a heavy toll. Perhaps that's one reason why some of the contributors to this volume, like me, speak of intentional community living in the past tense.

Mary Jo: There is a profound humility in those who bear witness in this book to the blessings and burdens of community. All refer to the human, flawed, and imperfect experiments that they have been part of. Nevertheless, they all acknowledge that while their efforts have not been perfect, they have been good. It is this ongoing search to do the good rather than the perfect, to be good rather than perfect, that is so inspiring. Not all these experiments succeeded or survived, but they each cast a measure of light and hope in their time. We Catholics who are tempted to think big and broad do well to heed such practical humility. All of us who believe we are called to community know that it can sometimes be an experiment in suffering and failure. To know this and to continue to follow this call is an experiment in hope.

This profound link between humility and hope is crucial for all of us who have honed our critique of the American empire. It is all too easy, as I have painfully discovered, to become like that which we are against. If our focus is primarily on who or what we are against, we will probably replicate those patterns within and among ourselves. Even small communities can replicate imperial dynamics within their local realities. Repentance and forgiveness are the way of humility and hope. Thus, we must focus our lives in terms of who and what we are *for*. The "following" of Christ is a lifelong task—a longer-than-life task—that concentrates our lives and makes them whole.

Ervin: Just as the Anabaptists of the sixteenth century insisted on a more faithful way to follow Jesus, these discipleship communities show important alternatives to traditional Christian churches. It is crucially important for traditional churches to see that the way of Christ does not begin or end with a North American way of doing things. Indeed, the heart of Anabaptism is a commitment to follow Jesus, no matter what the cost.

Anabaptism that accommodates the ways of the world is a contradiction in terms. Perhaps the best lesson I learned from the Amish community in which I grew up is that followers of Jesus are called to march to the beat of a different drummer. At times we need to "buck the system."

Reading these stories reminds me that there are people who are willing to make radical commitments in attempts to change the world. In most cases, that difference is reflected in both an inner and an outer journey. The inner journey is nurtured by a commitment to transformation of oneself through the insights and discipline exercised in communal interaction. The outer journey is a path toward a more just and peaceable world and is nurtured by a communal vision to make a difference in the world.

Mary Jo: Not all Christian communities can see an emperor a mile away; not all can see the long shadow of imperial power. However, reading these "Experiments in Christian Discipleship" is an astonishing exercise for those who have not been shaped by the Anabaptist experience. I was impressed by how many of these "experiments" took shape because of a spiritual insight into the "original sins" of empire: racism, violence, war, and the abuse of the environment and the outsider.

Such spiritual insight had immediate and practical conse-quences in terms of lifestyle and action. Where the empires imposed uniformity, the Anabaptists practiced community. The wisdom of the Anabaptist way is significant for all of us who live within the American empire, in this time and place that we call home. And, as several witnesses in this book point out, we know this empire well as it lives within us and among us. Other Christian denominations have their own wisdom about the way of community, but it is the Anabaptists who link their practice of community to their political discernment, to reading the signs of the times.

Ervin: The stories in this book demonstrate that many believers seek something substantial, something more authentic and real than the Christian world they see all around. They are willing to forsake the American dream for a way of life that promises justice and hope for those on the margins of society. It gives me hope that discipleship communities can indeed show the way for the world.

Mary Jo: All of these "experiments" suggest something about the future of the churches. I think that denominational differences will seem rather minor compared to the major choice that each Christian community has to make: Are we propping up the empire or are we participating in the building of the reign of God?

Mary Jo Leddy is founder of the Romero House Community in Toronto, Ontario, where she works alongside refugees. She is author of many books including: The Other Face of God: When the Stranger Calls Us Home *(Orbis 2011),* Our Friendly Local Terrorist *(Between the Line 2010), and* Reweaving Religious Life: Beyond the Liberal Model *(Twenty Third Publications 1990). She is adjunct professor of theology at Regis College, University of Toronto.*

Ervin R. Stutzman is a preacher, teacher, and writer. Before taking on his current role of Executive Director of Mennonite Church USA, in 2010, he served for nearly twelve years as Dean and Professor of Church Ministries at Eastern Mennonite Seminary, Harrisonburg, Virgina. His Herald Press publications include From Nonresistance to Justice: The Transformation of Mennonite Church Peace Rhetoric, 1908–2008 *and* Creating Communities of the Kingdom *(co-authored with David Shenk).*

INTRODUCTION

by Elaine Enns and Ched Myers

> *The true test of the Christian. . . is discipleship. The great word of the Anabaptists was not "faith" as it was for the reformers, but "following."*
> —Harold Bender, *The Anabaptist Vision*

Harold Bender's famous contention that discipleship stands at the center of distinctive Anabaptist identity has had influence well beyond the bounds of the Mennonite world. The "Anabaptist vision" has attracted increasing attention and conversation from churches across the ecumenical spectrum as post-Christendom realities cause them to rethink their faith and politics.

This anthology traces new and continuing expressions of this discipleship vision within, at the margins of, and wholly independent of the Mennonite church in North America over the last half century. This relational initiative to "widen the circle" arose from a conversation at an Interchurch Relations gathering of Mennonite Church USA in Akron, Pennsylvania, in the summer of 2008.[1] We were invited to reflect on the emergence of "new" peace and discipleship movements and their relationship with Mennonites, something we were delighted to do since this theme runs right through our marriage. Indeed, our experience is germane to the questions that shape this volume.

I.

Elaine was raised in the bosom of an active ethnic Mennonite community on the Canadian prairies, attending Mennonite schools from grade ten through college. Mennonite Voluntary Service then took her to Fresno, California, to work with a vibrant Victim Offender

Reconciliation Project. She stayed on to complete a graduate degree in Theology, Conflict Management and Peacemaking at Mennonite Brethren Biblical Seminary, and then to teach at the Center for Peacemaking and Conflict Studies at Fresno Pacific University. Elaine traces her deep interest in restorative justice to her grandparents, all four of whom were refugees from Russia and Ukraine in the 1920s in the wake of the horrific dispossession and murder of Mennonites during and after the Russian Revolution. She is grateful for an upbringing that was rich with good teaching, mentorship, and community (if also flawed by patriarchy and provincialism). As a result, a commitment to peace and justice is "in her bones."

In contrast, Californian Ched was not raised in any church, his father a lapsed Catholic, mother an ambivalent Episcopalian. He came to faith at eighteen as part of the "Jesus movement" of the late 1960s/early 70s, but shortly thereafter encountered the radical discipleship movement, whose motto was the "whole gospel for the whole person for the whole world." Ched was mentored by Catholic Workers, radical Baptists, Quakers, and faith-rooted activists of all stripes; participated in several intentional communities; and has worked for thirty-five years as an ecumenical peace and justice organizer and theologian.

Ched was one of many young evangelicals in the 1970s who discovered the Anabaptist vision through the work of John Howard Yoder, Harold Bender, and others. There he found a theological home, if not an ecclesial hearth. Denominationalism wasn't as important as discipleship to the community movement of that period (labeled in this volume as "Second Wave"). Renewal-oriented Lutherans, Methodists, Franciscans, or Congregationalists often had far more in common with each other than with their own less-engaged traditions. Still, Ched and others made attempts to find Mennonites with whom to be in conversation; too often, however, they experienced Mennonite institutions as insular and churches as less than hospitable to "mongrel outsiders" like him.

It wasn't until meeting Elaine that Ched had the opportunity to build relationships with ethnic Mennonites. The welcome was warm, though it has taken a while to get to know, and be known by, her clan. Yet Ched encountered in this community a deep spirituality and strength forged by suffering, which led him to complete the circle begun thirty-five years ago by recently joining the

Mennonite denomination. Here indeed was a river of faith and practice deep and broad enough to swim in.

Meanwhile, Elaine's immersion in Ched's extended radical discipleship network enabled her to live out more intensely her Anabaptist faith. She points as examples to four non-Mennonite discipleship communities which have had a tremendous impact on her:

1. The Open Door Community in Atlanta, Georgia, was begun by two Presbyterian ministers; members live and work with the homeless and advocate for those on Georgia's Death Row. This witness challenges Elaine to deepen and broaden her work in restorative justice.

2. Jonah House, in inner city Baltimore, Maryland, is a nonviolent resistance community in the Catholic Worker tradition, which for four decades has been on the forefront of prophetic witness against militarism and the nuclear arms race. The women elders of this community have inspired Elaine to greater courage in transforming patriarchy, and to take more seriously Paul's exhortation that the church preach the gospel to the Powers (Ephesians 3:10).

3. The Beloved Community Center is anchored in an African American Baptist congregation in Greensboro, North Carolina. BCC leaders have worked for racial and economic justice for decades, and helped launch the first Truth and Reconciliation Commission (TRC) on U.S. soil in response to the murder of five labor activists by white supremacists in 1979. Elaine's involvement with the Greensboro TRC has animated her to look at historical, political, and structural issues facing peacemaking work.

4. The Word and World People's School is an ecumenical and interracial collaborative founded in 2001 to provide alternative theological training for Christian disciples committed to the work of peace, social justice, and solidarity with the poor. Eight schools have been facilitated in different communities around the United States, as well as internships and a mentoring program. The "church as social movement" came alive for Elaine at these schools; she wishes more Mennonite youth could be exposed to this kind of discipleship education.

These and other discipleship communities embody convictions arrived at *not* through Anabaptist influences, but through Civil Rights organizing, solidarity with Latin America, nonviolent resistance to empire and war, and engagement with the poor and marginalized. Elaine felt welcomed by them, and learned the importance of celebration and mutual encouragement in the work of biblical justice and peacemaking in our violent world.

II.

With our experience in mind, we appealed to the participants at the Interchurch Relations consultation in Akron to be more proactive in building relationships with "new peace churches" and discipleship movements. This is an urgent mission task because we find ourselves at another historical moment of great opportunity for renewing and "widening the circle" of the Anabaptist vision, a moment both similar to and different from the 1970s, when Ched first encountered Anabaptism and radical discipleship.

Three broad trajectories are shaping this moment of flux in North American churches, each of which are reflected in the contributions to this volume:

1. *Dis-illusionment:* Through the Reagan-Bush eras, the Christian Right became a formidable sociological and political force, and arguably the dominant religious stratum in the United States, its backbone formed by white suburban evangelical megachurches. But this edifice is now crumbling, due to a variety of factors including hyper-politicization, internal contradictions, and relatively shallow theological moorings. Thousands of young people from this world—who have come of age under the shadow of global warming, resource wars, and deadening consumerism—are experiencing deep alienation from both their dysfunctional churches and society. Many are seeking more authentic, holistic, and *traditioned* models of faith and practice, and significant numbers are engaging Anabaptism (reflected in Chapters 12, 13, 15, 16, 17, and 19).

2. *Dis-establishment:* Meanwhile, leaders from atrophying mainstream Protestant denominations (as well as some Roman Catholics) are increasingly drawn to theologies of

discipleship, to gospel nonviolence, and to learning how to become truly post-Christendom churches. Both at the level of formal ecumenical conversation, and even more widely at the grassroots, Mennonites have become the subject of genuine interest. At the same time, many Mennonites are learning about prayer and liturgy from these other Christian traditions (as evidenced in Chapters 3, 5, 6, 7, 8, and 10).

3. *De-centering*: All North American denominations—including Mennonites—are experiencing the impact of changing demographics, which are steadily eroding "European" majorities. White male patterns of hegemony are being challenged by multicultural and post-colonial commitments, with issues of race, class, gender, and sexual orientation being raised persistently. In these matters Mennonites probably have more to learn from than to offer other traditions—but they are no less an opportunity for growth (see Chapters 1, 2, 4, 9, 11, 14, and 18).

Canadian theologian Douglas John Hall has written incisively about how the phenomenon of societal disillusionment (so widespread at present) represents a necessary condition to ecclesial renewal. In such a context, "the disciple community has the vocation of exploring the failure of the illusion that is passing, and of articulating a new expression of the faith which can absorb this failure and point toward a new symbolic transcendence of it."[2] These three trajectories thus represent "evangelical openings" for Mennonites, not only for promoting the gospel of discipleship among the religiously alienated, but also for partnerships with and mutual aid among kindred spirits and common public witness to God's dream of justice and peace.

We were delighted that the Akron consultation affirmed the need for intentional Mennonite outreach to, and hospitality toward, the various expressions of discipleship that have arisen in response to the above trends. This includes networking with established alternative communities such as those noted by Elaine; with the much-publicized "emergent" and "new monastic" movements; and with old and new expressions of racial-ethnic Christianity. André Gingrich Stoner, director of Interchurch Relations, soon hired a new staff person to explore this terrain, and Joanna Shenk immediately set about moving around the country, connecting with a wide variety of communities, and feeding back her findings to denominational colleagues.

An energetic young woman, Joanna has a keen eye and ear, strategic sensibility, and passionate commitment—just what is needed to facilitate this investigation of the intersection between "old" and "new" embodiments of the Anabaptist vision in a way that might animate both the U.S. Mennonite churches and other analogous discipleship movements. This collection represents the next step in this project, with the aim of advancing conversation among diverse voices and perspectives.

III.

In order to ensure that this volume would not be unwieldy, spatial and temporal delimitations were set early. On one hand, the focus is restricted to the North American context, acknowledging that this is only a subset of the wider transformations going on in the global church. On the other, the scope is limited to the last half-century of Mennonite and "Anabaptist-like" renewal movements. In the wake of World War II, this book identifies three "waves."

The first wave (Chapters 1–5) represents experiments forged during the difficult Cold War era of the 1950s and 60s. These pioneers are now our elders, and we owe them not only respect, but also our continuing, careful attention. Vincent and the late Rosemarie Harding's reflections on their work in Atlanta in the early sixties provide a fascinating and inspirational window into the Civil Rights movement (Chapters 1 and 2). Reba Place and the Lee Heights Community Church represent two other early expressions of Mennonite renewal that arose in relation to the Concern movement of the mid-50s (Chapters 3 and 4). And Canadian Hedy Sawadsky pioneered new peacemaking paths in relation to broader antiwar movements of the 60s and beyond (Chapter 5).

The second wave encompasses community experiments of the 1970s and 80s, as Ched has noted. Represented herein are two influential Washington, D.C., based organizations, Sojourners (Chapter 6) and Church of the Saviour, perhaps the longest running "missional church" experiment in North America (Chapter 8). The Bijou Street Community (Chapter 7) and Christian Peacemaker

Teams (Chapter 9) are examples of two different modes of Mennonite peacemaking. And James Nelson Gingerich explores the dialectic between maintenance and mission in a community-based health care center (Chapter 10).

Third wave expressions over the last two decades receive the most attention in this book and range from the traditional (Mennonite Voluntary Service, Chapter 11) to the innovative (Little Flowers Community, Chapter 16). Included are the testimonies of Christians who are moving toward Anabaptism (Chapter 13 and 15) and those moving away (Chapter 14); of white (Chapter 12) and Latino (Chapter 17) evangelicals exploring Mennonite identity; and reflections that are sociological (Chapter 18) and more lyrical (Chapter 19).

This collection provides diverse snapshots of recent incarnations of the Anabaptist vision about which Bender wrote. While many other communities could have been profiled, we believe this volume is representative of the various currents that are seeking to embody discipleship in contemporary North America. It could not come at a more propitious time as we approach the five hundredth anniversary of the Radical Reformation, and as all Christians face the multiple threats of intractable social disparity, rampant militarism, and the specter of ecological collapse. May this book help to animate and to resource an ever-widening circle of Anabaptist visionaries in this crucial historic moment.

Part One

FIRST WAVE
(1950s *and* 60s)

CHAPTER ONE

ANABAPTIST FORMATION:
An Interview with Vincent Harding

Conducted by Joanna Shenk

Civil Rights Movement leader Vincent Harding reflects on his relationship with the Anabaptist tradition and Mennonites since the late 1950s. In this interview he offers vision for Anabaptist-minded people today, as well as for all North American Christians. From friendship with Martin Luther King Jr. to mentorship of young people, Vincent challenges us to continue to create communities of love and justice.

What interested you in connecting with a Mennonite community in the first place? What was compelling to you about the Mennonite people and theology?

I was drafted into the U.S. Army when I was twenty-two years old, in 1953. I had finished college at Columbia University School of Journalism in New York City. Up to that point, the deepest religious impact on my life had come from the small church in Harlem, where I grew up.

They taught their young men to deal with the matter of military service, not in any way by calling up the possibility of conscientious objection but instead by calling people to go the way of the military, but not take up arms. But they did not focus on Jesus' teaching. They focused on "thou shalt not kill."

I continue to believe that the critical experience that I had in the military was in rifle practice at Fort Dix, New Jersey. I enjoyed firing a rifle very much and enjoyed becoming a good marksman.

I remember being down on my belly shooting at the target. It was almost as if someone was saying to me, "So you enjoy this, Vincent? So you think that's what the government is paying all this money for? So you can enjoy yourself shooting a rifle?"

It was really as if someone was saying, "No, that's not what they're paying for. You're being trained to kill a man without him even being able to see you. And what does that have to do with Jesus?"

Eventually, by the time I was ready to be discharged, I knew I was a conscientious objector.

I was still a part of my church and playing a significant role in its leadership. And as I wrestled with where to go to graduate school, having been accepted at Harvard, Yale, Columbia, and the University of Chicago, I found out that my church in Harlem had a mission church out in Chicago that needed a pastor.

It was while I was in Chicago that I kept wrestling with this whole matter of Jesus and my home church's emphasis on the Ten Commandments and not Jesus. At the University, I found out that there was such a thing as the history of Christianity. I started taking some courses at the divinity school and studying in the library there.

At the same moment, Elmer Neufeld, who was studying in the philosophy department, also used that library. Elmer was my first powerful contact with Mennonites. As I studied the history of Christianity, I had come across the Anabaptists. I had been deeply impressed by the fact that for hundreds of years, some people within the Christian faith had believed all the things that I had recently come to believe.

And then I met Elmer, who told me about this Mennonite congregation that had been organized around the Mennonite seminary in Chicago. He asked me if I was a part of any church and if I'd be interested in learning more about what they were doing. Elmer was chairperson of the trustees and Delton [Frantz] was the pastor at Woodlawn Mennonite Church. They asked me if I'd be willing to explore the possibility of being a copastor with Delton.

It came at a very propitious time. I was just at that time trying to write down for myself and for my home church a kind of statement explaining why I no longer believed what I had been raised to believe. It was quite a time of wrestling. Elmer's contact came just at that time. I had basically decided that I had to leave my home church and leave the church that I was supply pastoring in Chicago.

That was my entry into the Mennonite world, through Wood-lawn and the folks who were trying to organize Woodlawn church. As time went on I got to know more of the Mennonite folks around. People kept saying to me, "Well there's this Negro Mennonite girl that you ought to meet. She's over at Bethel Mennonite Church and we're sure you'll appreciate her very much." That was Rosemarie.

We finally did meet at a conference at Bethel. That was 1959. We were married in 1960.

Before connecting with Woodlawn, I did not have any strong idea of social justice or social service kinds of activities. And so the Wood-lawn experience was really the opening of that whole world to me—of the church having a mission in its community.

That was also really the first place where I was encouraged to explore the whole business of Christianity and race.

Prior to your coming, were people at Woodlawn wrestling with Christianity and race?

Yes. And they were trying to decide what it meant for this predomi-nately white group of folks based in the South Side of Chicago to try to develop a congregation that would be in the midst of an over-whelmingly black community—to try to translate white Mennonit-ism into the South Side of Chicago. All of those issues were actively a part of their coming into being.

So they invited me into that conversation and exploration.

Did you have a sense that what you were doing was different from what a lot of other Mennonites were doing in the United States?

From the time I started participating in the life at Woodlawn, I was constantly being invited to come out to other Mennonite places. I was, of course, reading Mennonite periodicals. So I was well aware that this was not the normal white Mennonite way of dealing with the issue of race.

I was well aware that many, many of the Mennonites were still carrying with them all the cultural and political fears that had driven them out from many places. And that in many cases to be the "still in the land"[1] was the way to be safe and secure. I was aware that many still saw this idea of obeying the powers that be as being the necessary way. And of course I was aware that many people saw whiteness as a protection from conflict and confusion and difficulties and chose not to come out from under that protection.

One example of Woodlawn's engagement with race and Christianity was a trip that you and four other men took through the South in 1958. That trip was the first time you met Dr. King, but I'm guessing you were all aware of his work?

Yes, everybody in the church leadership had been aware of King and especially the emphasis on nonviolence. It was basically through the Mennonite connections that I became sensitized to him and what he was trying to do.

For those of us on the trip—Elmer, Glen Bayes, Delton Frantz, Ed Riddick, and me—there was a profound sense of bonding. We all, of course, had to be very, very much afraid of what we were getting into. But at the same time, we had to get into it. It was so good that we could get into it together.

I guess everything about the trip, Joanna, was learning. There was no way not to learn. None of us had been in the South before.

It was while we were in southern Alabama that we had begun talking to ourselves about the fact that we shouldn't be in Alabama without trying to see Dr. King. So we just looked up King in the Montgomery phone book.

Coretta answered. We told her that we were traveling as an integrated group of guys from a church in Chicago. We'd be very honored if we could spend a little time talking to King. He was at that point recuperating from a stab wound that he had received while he was on a book tour—*Stride Toward Freedom*.

When we got there, she was so glad and surprised to see the five of us together. So she went in and he was in bed in his pajamas. She came back out and said, "My husband would very much like to see you."

And you visited in his bedroom?

Yes. Some of us sat around in chairs, but I was sitting on the bed. He was just his beautiful self. He was kidding with us. He immediately was congratulating us on making it through Mississippi. [laughing]

So, at the end of the visit, he then invited you to come to the South and work with the movement. What was it like to receive that invitation?

Powerful and moving. And I saw it as a kind of special word not only to us but to Mennonites, because he looked at Ed [also a black man] and me and said, "Now you guys, you're Mennonites and you know something about nonviolence. You understand what we're trying to do down here. You ought to come back down here and help us."

So he knew something about Mennonites.

[In 1961 the Hardings moved to Atlanta to create and lead Mennonite House. For more on Mennonite House, see Chapter 2 by Rosemarie Freeney Harding.]

How did the Mennonite "powers that be" respond to the evolution of the Mennonite House into a "movement" house and not just a place for volunteers to live?

I think some people had to wrestle with it. Some people in the leadership understood immediately the importance of that kind of concrete manifestation of sisterhood and brotherhood and discipleship. Some were very leery about getting in trouble with the police or with any kind of violent racist that might be around. Most of what we heard, although we didn't have a great deal of contact with them, was coming from the southern-based Mennonite churches. They didn't want us to come close.

That certainly would have been the case if we had been representing certain kinds of Methodists or Baptists or others, who were essentially white and grounded in the white way of life in the South. But there were exceptions. And one of my favorite exceptions was Titus Bender. He was head of a voluntary service center in Meridian, Mississippi.

Mennonite Central Committee (MCC) tried when we first went there to pull together people who had MCC connections at a conference, I think, in Nashville. Titus came and we agreed that it would be a very important witness to the South, to the church, to our lives, for us to come and visit him in Meridian.

And Titus, bless his heart, told us it was probably not a good idea to get into town and be asking about how to get to where they lived. But we agreed that there was a filling station just off the highway as we entered the Meridian area and that we should stop there and use the telephone.

That's really one of my [pause for tears] favorite memories.

We got to the filling station. It was daytime. And there was the usual filling station cast of characters sitting around. Talking, looking, seeing what the day held. When we pulled up, they were looking at us. We made the call and they were still looking at us. Pretty sure that Rose was still wearing a covering at the time.

When Titus came he decided that it was an appropriate and important and necessary thing to share with me a Mennonite hug and kiss. [chuckling] I'm glad he was not crazy enough to do it to Rose. It was bad enough for me. And so the folks looked.

Then we followed him to his place. And he always jokes about the fact that their next-door neighbors suddenly found the need for all kinds of things. "Could they borrow some sugar?" [laughing] They sent the children over. . . they had about three borrowing visits.

It was a wonderful act of courage.

And that was also the time when you began working closely with Dr. King, connecting with the broader movement?

We were right around the corner from them. That was very powerful. Rose and Coretta became very close to each other. Martin started asking us to come to various places where SCLC (Southern Christian Leadership Conference) was carrying on its campaigns. From a variety of connections, we came very close to the young people in SNCC (Student Nonviolent Coordinating Committee). We worked with them in a number of places. And sometimes, some of them stayed at Mennonite House.

It was clear that a major part of our responsibility in the South was to interpret to the Mennonite churches around the country and the world what was going on and why Mennonites should be concerned about it.

Some were saying, "Thank you very much for illuminating us." Some were saying, "We want to find a better direction than we've been going. Help us." And some were saying, "No thank you, not this time."

What was it that gave you and Rosemarie the passion, the energy, the desire to continue to relate in those years, in the 1960s, particularly when you were receiving varied responses from Mennonites? What compelled you to continue to connect, given the resistance?

Part of it was the Titus Benders and Elmer Neufelds of the church. We knew that there were people who were deeply concerned, some of whom were willing to make great sacrifices to change the church and the country. And those became, in many cases, very deep, loving, and rewarding friendships. That was the ground on which we stood.

We were quite certain that at its best, the "Anabaptist vision," (as Harold Bender called it) was something that was good for us all. Including Anabaptists.

You worked with King to draft the "Beyond Vietnam" speech that he delivered at Riverside Church on April 4, 1967, exactly one year before his assassination. Did you influence his thinking about Vietnam? Or was that something that he had been wrestling with already?

It was part of him. And he'd been speaking for several years before the 1967 speech and we were quite aware of what each other thought about this and how deeply we were connected to it. He knew that there was going to be some flack, but he didn't know how much there was going to be.

We made a very courageous decision.

[Harding did research related to the Vietnam War in Chicago while living at Reba Place Fellowship in 1964–65 while finishing his PhD at Chicago University. This was following the time in Atlanta with Mennonite House.]

That was one of the great gifts of the stay at Reba Place because, along with the Reba community, I had many ongoing discussions on the war and what it meant for Christians especially. That was a very important context for me to bring with me when I went back to Atlanta [to teach at Spelman College]. After I accepted the offer to teach, somehow I knew that I should not go without knowing more about Vietnam.

Reba Place presented a very good opportunity. I think I spent just about the whole summer of 1965 before going back to Atlanta getting immersed in the materials on Vietnam.

That was another important contribution that came from the Mennonite connections. One of the things I referenced was a whole set of reports from MCC workers in Vietnam and what their experiences were as the war built up.

On a timeline of your work I noticed there was a gradual shift from the work you had been doing in the Mennonite world, to a more intentional focus related to Dr. King's work and related to the founding of the Institute of the Black World. Was there a shift you experienced in those years that oriented your focus in a new way?

That period from 1966 to 1970 or so was a very powerful period for any of us who were deeply connected to the life of the black community and especially to the struggles of the black community.

I tend not to use the word *shift* too easily. I see a development, a movement. All over the black community, people were exploring and discovering their own deepest cultural roots. And that was the case for me. That whole period of Black Power, Black Consciousness, Black Culture was a period of deepening introspection and discovery. I remember during that time I was talking with Staughton and Alice Lynd who had been friends since my earliest Atlanta days. He was still teaching at Spelman College at the time.

I was telling them about a kind of hesitation I had of moving too deeply into the world of blackness and wondering how that would affect my life and the world of Christian faith. Alice said she really didn't think that I had to worry. She had a sense that the God who had taken me deep into Christian faith could also take me deep into Blackness and not leave me.

But it was a time when a lot of my Mennonite friends weren't quite sure how to read where I was and where I was going. I remember more than one piece of correspondence that said in so many words, "Are you still a part of us? Do you still belong to us?" I remember there was a time when I had to depend upon the fact that those with whom I had developed a deep personal loving connection would understand where I was maybe even more than I understood myself and would not feel that they had to keep some kind of grip on me—and would not feel that I had to be in the same kind of relationship with them as I had been in the past.

I know that there was a period in this time of Blackness when I felt I needed to stand in the heart of the black community, partly because I had been given the gift of learning and knowing and receiving many things that many people in the black community had not been able to experience. That was part of my Anabaptist understanding of life and faith—especially the whole matter of trying to take Jesus seriously.

Now I'm sure that many people would use the word *shift* to characterize my movement in that period. I see it more as a deepening, expanding, exploring. Watering the roots.

As you were deepening and expanding, you were writing for a broad range of audiences, not just Mennonite. So were certain people confused about how to locate you within the Mennonite story?

That's a good thing to try to clarify. I have recently been in my materials at the Emory archives and was fascinated by what I was writing for the Mennonite community. And the fact is that that audience was one of my first major audiences as I started writing on issues of faith and action.

But even in that early period I was also doing things for other publications. Once we went south, we were taking as one significant element of our responsibility the need to try to help Mennonites understand what was going on in the South. So it was very natural to write for and to Mennonites what we understood to be taking place.

At the same moment, there were lots of other people who we needed to address about what was taking place. There were some Mennonites that sort of felt, "This is our Negro. And we're just happy to have him talking to us even though we don't always listen. But you know, he's talking to us."

But then when "their Negro" started talking to others as well, or sometimes didn't seem to talking to them anymore at all, there was this kind of feeling that "he doesn't like us anymore, he left us, he's not our Negro anymore."

People, I'm sure, did not identify that kind of feeling consciously, but obviously it was very important to them.

One of the things I used to do in writing (and I remember part of it was quite consciously chosen, but it confused some people): I used to speak again and again about "we Mennonites" and what "we" have to think about. It was clearly a way of saying, "You cannot distance yourself from me because I'm black. I am speaking from within the community and this is my community."

It was a conscious choice to identify myself with those who did not always know how to identify with me.

What I've recognized is how much my life was really affected by the connection with the Mennonite church communities. I was learning and teaching in that setting. I was identifying with that setting. And I'm sure that the whole Black Consciousness period caused me to be increasingly sensitive to the dangers of being somebody's Negro.

I think that was a very important preparation for me to go south and to participate in all the struggles and dialogues that grew out of the Black Consciousness period. I had this real connection to a community where there was at least the potential of people really loving each other across racial lines, and I had come to the point with some of my Mennonite sisters and brothers where I could wrestle with them around these issues because we had assumed a kind of family relationship.

I know from that point on, that's always been one of my goals and one of the things I try to help others to move toward: To take all the risks that are involved in getting to a kind of familial relationship with people across racial lines. To get messy and connected and involved and angry and sorrowful and everything else that deeply engaged people are supposed to get.

What I discovered was that love trumps ideology every time. And that was certainly the case with my Mennonite deepest, dearest friends.

Whenever Titus called, I was there.

The connections are created out of struggle and they are not easily overcome. Obviously, there are sometimes exceptions, but by and large, that is not easily lost. So I felt that way about many of the folks with whom I had lived and worked in the Mennonite faith community.

They would have then been people who weren't afraid of the growth, the change, the conflict. What does holistic, active peacemaking look like?

It looks like a lot of wrestling with the angels. That's what it looks like. [*laughter*]

And you get crippled in the process and you're never the same again. But you can't run away from that and be whole.

What observations or thoughts do you have about Mennonites in this larger context of North American Christianity?

Well, Joanna, I think there are certain interesting parallels between what Mennonites have in their history to serve as a resource, if it is desired, and what American Christians have in our history, if it is desired as a resource.

As I had mentioned to you yesterday, one of the most important things that drew me to the Mennonites was the early Anabaptists.

What I knew was that, at their best, they were constantly driving toward the goal of taking Jesus seriously and not letting anything get in the way of that. Especially taking his counter-cultural callings seriously. And in many ways, taking his counter-*religious* teachings seriously—about dealing with enemies, about dealing with possessions, about dealing with hunger and thirst for righteousness.

All those things, it seemed to me, bring into the center of the discussion the meaning of following Jesus as a disciple who sees the cross as absolutely normal to a way of living. All of that, for me, was of great significance and I found that in dealing with Mennonites, some were more connected to that history than others. I found that some, of course, not only remembered Jesus, but remembered their own experience of "underdog-ness." Of course, as you know, there are two or three basic ways of dealing with our history when we've been underdogs.

One of them is to get as far away from underdog status as we can and to get as far away from anyone who is in that status. Another one is to grab them and hold them and say, "I know you and I live this, and I'm not going to let you live it by yourself."

And Mennonites at least had a choice. They knew what [the second way] was about if they knew their history. And so, that was for me a very important resource that the church could bring into the situation of racism, race and white supremacy, and black underdog-ness in American society. These understandings are gifts that are available to Mennonites if they are ready to take the risks of those gifts.

All followers of Jesus carry this long tradition that seems to have begun with the earliest Christians of being always in tension with the imperial powers of the time. There is something within us, when we are at our best, which makes for a struggle with imperial domination—whether it's racial domination, cultural domination, economic domination, certainly military domination. We have this tremendous history of being terribly uncomfortable with that rule. So much of our earliest Christian characteristics came out of living in tension with the powers that be. I think that one of the beautiful challenges of this time is to do some deep reflection on what it means to be embedded in the life of an imperial power that also sees itself as a democratic society, therefore placing responsibility for the power on all of us and offering a peculiar challenge to those of us who say we are followers of the ones who were killed by the empire.

And now we become chaplains and cheerleaders of the empire. How do we wrestle with that? What do we have to do to find our way through that terrible dilemma? I think that for young people especially who see themselves connected to some kind of Anabaptist version of the Christian stories, it is quite an invitation to figure out the kind of life you have to live if you're going to stay in tension with the mainstream.

I remember one twenty-first century theologian from California defining the Christian life as a life of creative insecurity.

So I think that younger people especially, who are being shaken out of the nefarious securities of faith and economics and culture and race and everything else, are being offered a magnificent chance to see if that business of creative insecurity is something more than just a fascinating phrase.

I think that they are really being offered this opportunity to see if there is still any life, any significance, anything rich and especially challenging to the Anabaptist traditions. So much in this culture seems geared to drive us away from those kinds of values.

It's even more important for there to be some strange people around, who are saying through their lives, "There is another way to be."

CHAPTER TWO
ATLANTA'S MENNONITE HOUSE

By Rosemarie Freeney Harding with Rachel Harding

Rosemarie Freeney Harding was a 1955 graduate of Goshen College, a Mennonite educational institution. Along with her spouse Vincent Harding, Rosemarie co-led the first interracial Mennonite Voluntary Service Unit in Atlanta, Georgia, from 1961 to 1964. This unit, Mennonite House, served as a home for volunteers and a place of hospitality for Civil Rights leaders from across the southern United States. This chapter is adapted from Rosemarie's yet-to-be-published memoir, Remnants: A Spiritual Memoir, *finished by her daughter Rachel following her passing in 2004.*

Black people in Atlanta were intrigued with Mennonite House. This was something new—an interracial social service project tied to the freedom movement, where most of the volunteers were white and the directors were black, and everybody lived together in the same house. In 1961, this was definitely new. Seeing my husband and me in the leadership roles made black folks glad and proud. And it impressed them to know that our church (which most had never heard of) had sent us to represent the denomination. I didn't realize the significance of all this until later. I was just happy to be there.

We moved to Atlanta in the fall. The student sit-ins had been developing for a little over a year and freedom movement campaigns were spreading to cities and rural communities all across the South. With the Southern Christian Leadership Conference (SCLC) and the Student Nonviolent Coordinating Committee (SNCC) both headquartered in Atlanta, the city was a major administrative center for movement work—and in comparison to some other places in the region, it was a little less regressive in its racial politics. No one knew exactly what all the social and political changes would mean—especially how white people would react. But we were excited and, despite some fear, most blacks yearned for the transformations the movement was bringing.

Vincent and I came south to be a part of this. We were married the year before in Chicago, my hometown, where Vincent was serving as a lay pastor at Woodlawn Mennonite Church, finishing his PhD and where I was teaching at Brown Elementary School. We were both Mennonites, but my husband was a member of the General Conference and I was Old Mennonite. I had come to the denomination through my sister Alma and the Westside Chicago Bethel Mission Church. Vincent learned of the Mennonites from friends at the University of Chicago divinity school. Both of us were strongly attracted to the Anabaptist emphasis on peace and reconciliation and we had each been addressing churches and attending conferences on the rising southern freedom movement. So, before we even met, people were telling us about each other, noticing the similarities in our interests and thinking that we would be a good pair.

After we married, we convinced Mennonite Central Committee (MCC) that the church should have a presence in the southern movement. They agreed and gave Vincent and me the task of designing and coordinating that presence in line with MCC's longstanding tradition of voluntary service work. We followed the general model of Christian service in a context of faith-based community living, but our project was unique in its emphasis on racial justice and reconciliation in the U.S. context. Volunteers were invited to come in a spirit of sharing, a spirit of service, and with an openness to living and working toward justice with many kinds of people. Vincent and I were the first African American directors of an MCC service unit anywhere in the country and our work was closely observed, and, I think, largely applauded.

But Mennonite House was more than just a place where black and white volunteer workers lived. And it was more than an administrative center for their placement with various social service and activist organizations. The house was also a kind of community center—providing a space for people to gather, debate, and reflect on what was happening around us in the movement. It was even an urban retreat space of sorts, a space of welcome for activists who needed safe haven.

With the help of a black real estate agent, we found and quickly rented the two-story, white frame house at 540 Houston Street which had once belonged to the family of the great concert singer, Mattiwilda Dobbs. The first floor had a kitchen, a large living room, a dining room, a sitting room, and a little study that we turned into a bedroom. Upstairs were three or four more bedrooms with two or three beds in each. At our normal capacity, we easily sheltered twelve people, and when necessary, we put a curtain in the downstairs sitting room and a cot on the landing between the first and second floor to house even more.

Not all of the young people who lived and worked with us were Mennonites, but the majority of the volunteers came from Mennonite communities in the Midwest and Canada. Many had recently finished college and were members of congregations that encouraged church-based service work. They were also attracted to the movement and wanted to be involved in something that was helping our country fulfill its ideals. And they did well, these young white men and women. We held regular household meetings to talk about the voluntary service assignments and household issues, and every weekend we cleaned. It really worked out well. Our volunteers became friends and neighbors to people in the black community where we lived and they worked for black organizations and social service agencies. This was all very new and completely different from what most of them had known before.

When we first got to the city, one of my responsibilities was to make contacts with local groups who might employ our volunteers. I would explain our intentions and talk to them about the Mennonites. I told people we weren't looking for paid income for the volunteers, that the church was taking care of that. (MCC provided stipends of about fifteen dollars per month. There were also allowances for Vincent and me and for the upkeep of the house.) All the black groups we approached were very willing to have our volunteers work with them. At that time, black people were quite open to living and working more equally with whites. They welcomed the opportunity, and a few of the white ones did as well.

I placed volunteers with nursery schools, orphanages, community centers, day camps, Goodwill Industries, and some movement organizations like SCLC. The task of coordinating the service internships was, in a sense, an extension of the social work I had done in Chicago. But this was even more exciting because whites did not normally work in the places where we were sending these young people. At least, they did not work under black people's supervision. This was part of what made everyone so keenly interested in what Mennonite House was doing.

The Koinonia Partners community was one of the inspirations for Mennonite House.[1] After we arrived in Atlanta, we visited Koinonia often and developed a wonderful friendship with Clarence and Florence Jordan and other members of the farming fellowship. We also had friends among the founders of the Reba Place Fellowship in Evanston, Illinois, a group of young Anabaptist activists trying to live a practice of community and service. The tradition of hospitality and welcome from my own family was another strong influence on Mennonite House. The presence of our daughter, Rachel, who was born in 1962, and my nephew, Charles, who was a volunteer in the movement and lived with us at many points over the years, helped emphasize the family atmosphere in the house.

A houseful of friendly white neighbors

When we were first settling in, Edgar Metzler, head of the MCC Peace Section, came down for a few days to help us. Edgar asked me to go with him to greet our neighbors and inquire if they minded an integrated group of volunteers living next door. I told him I'd be happy to go, but his question was odd to me. I wouldn't have thought to ask it. Maybe it was a question that needed to be asked of whites, but I knew black people would be honored, because we want togetherness so much. . . at least, all the black people I know love justice and peace and we *really* wanted that then. The people who lived around us sympathized with what we were doing and were very supportive. On one side there was a family and on the other, an older lady who lived by herself. She was well-to-do and thought the idea of a houseful of friendly white neighbors was heavenly.

Back then, because of segregation, black people of different economic statuses lived very near each other. So our neighborhood was home to both wealthy and working class people. We had heard that the woman in the house across the street wasn't very sociable. She rarely left her home except to get in her large car and drive away, and she hardly ever smiled at anyone. Well, she must have been glad to have us in the neighborhood because she would come out and stand on her porch and watch us from time to time, smiling and nodding our way.

Neighborhood people were stopping by almost daily, just to visit, to talk—sometimes bringing gifts or donating furniture, and always wanting to know more about who we were and what we were doing. They liked the positive environment at Mennonite House; they would tell us this. We were demonstrating integration right in front of them. As people realized what we were trying to do, everybody wanted to help.

Young people were especially curious. There was a high school diagonally across the street and once the students discovered us, some dropped by every day on their way home. They were reading things in the news about changes and challenges in the country, and here was something in their own neighborhood that they could watch and participate in and feel connected to. One young woman began coming over so often that she took to spending the nights in our guest room.

Some of the volunteers who came to Mennonite House stayed for a year or more. Others spent just two or three months or a summer. Then there were a few people, like Septima Clark and my nephew Charles, who lived and worked with us for much of the period that we directed the project. Septima was running the Citizenship Education program of SCLC when she stayed with us, and Charles was assisting her. She could have lived anywhere but I think she just loved the idea, the concept, of Mennonite House and she wanted to be a part of it. There were other movement folks who came for only a day or for a few nights as they passed through on their way to destinations elsewhere in the region.

Visitors and conversations: What sort of beautiful nation we could create

One of our housemates was a master carpenter who built a large wooden table for the dining room. We had some of the best conversations around that homemade table. People like Staughton and Alice Lynd[2] came by, not only to lecture but just to talk with whoever was there. Howard Zinn[3] did the same—sometimes giving a presentation, but just as often joining the discussion. Andy and Jean Young[4] came also. They had moved to the city around the same time as me and Vincent and we got to know each other well in the movement days. The house would be so full that all the places at the table were taken and people would stand or bring in chairs to make room for everyone who wanted to be there.

All kinds of people came. I think folks were incredibly intrigued by this group of black and white people living together. It was a novelty. But it was also something that lots of people took as a sign of promise. Even remembering it now, I feel that same elation, that same sense of possibility. It was a moment of immense hope— immense hope in the whole country. People were trying all kinds of positive things to see what sort of beautiful nation we could create.

I remember the Muslims came too—people from the Nation of Islam—and they'd participate in the discussions. I went to some of the meetings at their temple, as well. They were always very thoughtful and polite in all of our interactions. I have very good memories of them. One man who visited us several times was Lonnie X. Cross; he was head of the math department at Atlanta University back in the early sixties. He's now Abdulalim Abdullah Shabazz. I got to know him well and I respected him a great deal. People from the Nation were interested in what it really meant for blacks and whites to live together, so they came by our house to see. There was a lot of talk among African Americans about *Blackness* and *Black Power*, but underlying all of it was a great concern for fairness, for reconciliation, for justice. Those were the things we discussed around that table and in many other places where black people got together. We talked about *peace*. The Muslim brothers and sisters were there, so it wasn't as if they were closed to those ideas, otherwise they would not have visited us and they would not have been interested in what we were doing.

Mennonite House was around the corner from where Martin and Coretta King lived and we became good friends in those years— working together and living nearby. Our focus on nonviolence and religiously-based reconciliation resonated with the Kings, who were already deeply committed to those values and were happy to discover more companions on that way. Martin came by the house sometimes, but he was busier and traveling a great deal, so, usually, Coretta would just come on her own. She'd sit and talk with the volunteers or visit with me and the baby, Rachel. Coretta was pregnant herself then, with her youngest daughter, Bunny. I think she found our little community house relaxing, maybe even a bit of a refuge. It must have been a solace to have sympathetic people—black and white together—with whom to share what was going on in her life. I remember once or twice she talked about the insulting telephone calls and threatening letters they received. But Coretta's conversation was more often on the potential of the movement and the encouragement coming from people all around the country and the world. Mostly, she had a real sense of peace about her. An assurance. Like all of us, she must have felt fear at times, but she never let it overwhelm her.

Refuge and reconnaissance

Mennonite House was also a place where movement people came, seeking a retreat, a little rest and distance from the frontlines. They were depressed by what they had experienced, or just exhausted and feeling discouraged. Sometimes the people who came to us had been assaulted or terrorized. Fannie Lou Hamer[5] came after she was brutally attacked in Wynona, Mississippi. Badly bruised and swollen, she was afraid to go home, worried that her husband might put himself in danger if he saw her condition. So Andy Young, James Bevel, and Dorothy Cotton[6] brought Mrs. Hamer to Mennonite House for a few days. Sometimes our friends at Koinonia would call us and say, "This young man, or this young woman, needs to just stay with y'all for a little bit." And we would take them in and they would stay with us until they felt stable. The atmosphere at Mennonite House was homey and respectful and full of enthusiasm about the movement. So it was a good place for visitors who needed some extra encouragement.

We had such a strong commitment to the movement and to integration. And we tried to reflect that not only in the voluntary service projects and in our communal life at Mennonite House, but also, as much as possible, in our interactions with public institutions and private businesses as well. Most of the doctors we saw were black, and we went to a black hospital for emergencies. The black doctors easily accepted the white volunteers who needed to be treated for colds or sprains or other illnesses they suffered during their time with us. But we were also trying to find white doctors who were ready to serve a racially mixed clientele. Initially, Vincent and I were the only blacks in the household and it wasn't so easy to find white professionals who would attend us. Looking back on it now, I don't know if it was even such a good idea for us to try this experiment while I was pregnant.

I was nervous, new to the city, and having my first child away from my family. At first, I was willing to try. My husband and I both genuinely believed in doing whatever we could do to push the barriers back and offer a challenge to segregation. . . but I had my doubts about this project. One of our friends, a white Quaker, had recommended a doctor to us. "He's excellent," the friend said, so we made an appointment.

When Vincent and I arrived at the office, no one spoke to us. We sat in the waiting room, surrounded by the doctor's white patients, but no one greeted us. There were a few hard stares and muttered comments, but mostly we received a studied inattention, the quiet of indignation. The receptionist was very curt and we sat in the stony chill of the room until we were called to see the physician. He was so distressed, he trembled slightly and his hands were damp as he examined me. It was awful. "Listen," I said to him after a short while, "I can see you're uncomfortable. I don't want to upset you and I don't want you to upset me, because all this might be affecting my baby. Maybe we should just cancel the appointment. I'll find someone else." He seemed to catch himself then, and tried to summon a confidence that neither he nor I felt. After that visit I decided I wouldn't go back. I didn't need the stress.

But about a week later, the doctor called to apologize. He didn't have his nurse or receptionist call; he called himself and said he was sorry and that I'd be welcome at his office if I cared to return. I said to myself, if he could take that step, I would honor it and reciprocate. But I wondered if the friend who referred us had considered whether this doctor had ever seen black patients or whether he would be uncomfortable—or maybe the doctor himself hadn't known what his own reaction would be. After a few visits, he was much less stilted with me and we started having conversations about Mennonite House and some of the work we were doing there. And he delivered my daughter when she was born.

Actually, we met many people who were trying to have a positive attitude about integration. But there were also situations where we encountered problems. Once, a Canadian couple was approached by a group of roughneck white youths in a park on the north side. The couple was babysitting Rachel while Vincent and I were out of town, and the boys surrounded and threatened them as they held my young child in their arms. "This park is for white people," the boys said. They told the couple that the black baby was not welcome in the park and told them to leave. When the Canadians explained that they were caring for the daughter of friends and that we all lived together, the boys were even more livid. "Why do you want to do that?" they wanted to know. "We don't believe in that, and it's an insult to white people."

Later, when our friends reported what had happened, it gave me so much to think about. I hadn't realized that many white people saw the freedom movement as a *personal* affront. Of course I recognized the structural resistance to change that racism created. But it slowly dawned on me that what we in the movement viewed as acts of justice, acts of freedom, acts of Christian community, were perceived by many whites as personal offenses and threats to their entitlements. Their reactions were reactions of anger, frustration, and the violence of spoiled children. The young men in the park eventually backed down because of the way our friends responded—talking about what they believed and how they were trying to live those beliefs. The Canadian couple had a kindness that I think disarmed the youths somewhat.

In this, Koinonia was an important example for us. They went through tremendous struggles, great hardships, to live an inclusive vision of their faith and to make their personal lives consistent with what they were preaching. Whenever we visited the farm, we would leave with more clarity about our own work—the movement work, the voluntary service work. Koinonia reminded us that the emphasis should be on service. Sharing not only your goods with others, but your whole life.

The importance of Mennonite House was its existence at a time when the student movement was taking off and people were coming to Atlanta from all over the country to join in the effort to transform our nation into its best image of itself. In the early 1960s, Mennonite House was one of the places, perhaps one of the few, where

interracial conversation and community were being consciously created in the South. Our work encouraged that impulse in the life of
the city of Atlanta and in the life of the freedom movement.

CHAPTER THREE

REBA PLACE FELLOWSHIP:
An Evolving Movement

by Sally Schreiner Youngquist and Celina Varela

*As one of the oldest Christian intentional communities in the
United States, Reba Place Fellowship (RPF) has much wisdom
and experience to offer. Current RPF leader Sally Schreiner
Youngquist outlines different periods in Reba's history, while
Celina Varela offers perspectives as a newer member of the
Reba community. Together these two women, in historical and
narrative form, provide glimpses into life at Reba Place.*

I, Sally, joined Reba Place Fellowship in 1973, attracted to the
stable discipleship community with a fifteen-year track record. In
the midst of the anti-Vietnam War movement and hippie era, communal living experiments were springing up all over the country.
But this Anabaptist group was different: they presented me with a
model of ethically responsible Christian singles and married couples sharing property and raising families in an interracial neighborhood south of the university I attended. Unlike most people in
my affluent suburban background, they lived frugally, practiced
pacifism, worshipped without a formal church building, organ, or
American flag, and pooled their incomes so more was available to
share with others.

I was one of sixteen college-aged peers who had launched our
own trial experiment in intentional Christian community the previ-
ous year. As graduation approached, most of the group dispersed.
Having one more semester of student teaching to finish, I stuck

around. Our RPF landlords invited the remnant from our group to explore God's call to join forces with them. I desired support in transitioning from college to the adult work world as I looked for teaching jobs. So I joined the intentional neighbors' class, began attending a weekly small group, and became convinced that if I were serious about following Jesus, I could find no better group than this one to accompany me. Since joining, I feel as if I've been part of at least five successive communities, with a thread of continuity joining all of them together. Many with whom I started have left, but among the forty-three covenant members, twelve old-timers remain whose memberships preceded mine.

Laying the foundation (1957–1972)

The community arose out of the Concern movement launched by Mennonite graduate students in post-World War II Europe who were sobered by the cultural assimilation of the European Mennonite churches. They felt "the recovery of the Anabaptist Vision" articulated by Harold S. Bender would not take the North American Mennonite churches far enough back to the radical roots of church life described in the book of Acts. RPF founder John Miller was sent on leave from his teaching post at Goshen Biblical Seminary so that his idealism could be tempered by experience within the traditional church. Instead, he took this opportunity to move to nearby metro Chicago in 1957 and put his student groups' ideals into practice. RPF formed as a community of love witnessing to the cultural idols of Mars (war), Mammon (materialism), and Me (individualism). When I arrived at the end of the first era, the group was small enough to share worship and meals on the first floor of the house at 727 Reba Place.

Accommodating rapid growth and Spirit-empowered ministry (1973–1979)

Six evangelicals from my student group became the first wave of baby boomers to swell the ranks of RPF. Openness to charismatic renewal contributed to the rapid growth of RPF from forty adult members to 150 in six years' time. We were challenged to recognize the elders operating in our midst and give them authority to lead.

Encouraged by the model of Church of the Redeemer in Houston, Texas, we developed large extended-family ministering households in our three-story Victorian houses and adjacent apartment buildings. Many seeking healing for broken marriages, addictions, and deep trauma from the past were welcomed. Worship life flourished with members creating music, dance, drama, and art. Weddings abounded and children multiplied. Lacking the necessary maturity, wisdom, and experience, however, we took on more than we could handle. We made mistakes with over-authoritarian approaches to pastoral care, hurt one another, and experienced fallout.

An Episcopal mentor challenged us to be more submitted and connected to the wider body of Christ. Acknowledging our tendencies toward self-righteousness and looking to our Anabaptist roots, we joined the Church of the Brethren and the Mennonite Church in 1975-76, though less than half of us came from these backgrounds. At the same time, we formalized relationships with other intentional communities with whom we had close ties as our primary affiliation. This group became known as the Shalom Covenant, later renamed Shalom Mission Communities. This remains the community's primary circle of accountability in giving and seeking counsel.

After discovering the effort required to keep up with two denominations, we later dropped back to sole affiliation with the Mennonite Church. This has provided some good cross-pollination. We have shared many gifts with the wider denomination—people and worship resources, hospitality to visitors, models of ministry, and participation in wider mission efforts. From the denomination we have received credentialing of pastors and added respectability, Christian education curriculum, hymnals, use of camps and higher education institutions, wider missional connections, and many rich friendships crossing urban/rural and cultural divides. For many in RPF, the denominational connection is peripheral, seen more as a theological rootage than an ongoing source of shared life.

Diversifying options for participation (1980–89)

A much-needed time of review, reflection, repentance, and regrouping followed the large household era. We recognized the need to grant more autonomy to those for whom communal life had become less than voluntary. Most families raising children opted to return to nuclear family living arrangements. The shared living households which continued became smaller and less complex. We reaffirmed our understanding that communal sharing was not a biblical requirement. It could be a barrier in reaching African American neighbors or including those worshipping among us who were not feeling called to these particular disciplines. Leaders valuing less-structured ways of sharing life and accountability offered to pioneer the establishment of a congregational membership option. After much discussion and discernment, Reba Place Church was birthed from Reba Place Fellowship in 1980. The congregational sector grew rapidly and multiplied into additional clusters while RPF's two communal clusters went into slow decline in numbers. Male elders from both sectors provided church oversight.

During this period I sought a more outward-directed mission experience with Mennonite Central Committee, asking to be sent as a representative of RPF. Leading the Atlanta voluntary service unit and then working in U.S. program administration provided me with good leadership development. Such experiences drew out pastoral gifts, but I wanted more training. So after discernment with the RPF home base, I enrolled in seminary at Associated Mennonite Biblical Seminary in Elkhart, Indiana.

While I can admit to discouragement about the viability of intentional Christian community during the low points of our past, I never questioned my basic covenant commitment to membership in Reba Place Fellowship. When I arrived back at RPF in 1984, we were into another divisive round of discussion on men's and women's roles in church leadership. I got the chance to preach, lead worship, and join the administrative team of RPC as we experimented with new patterns. I felt vulnerable to be in a pioneering role, but also empowered by God and affirmed by many of my sisters and brothers. I found it important to exhibit a peaceful spirit toward people holding the gamut of opinions on this issue (both men and women). Even with differences existing among us, I was licensed and eventually ordained to the ministry at RPC along with some of my male colleagues.

Discerning and supporting new missional directions (1990–1999)

In a quest toward greater evangelistic outreach and racial reconciliation with our neighbors, we called an African American pastor to join the church's pastoral team. This resulted in greater inclusion of African American leaders and worship gifts in RPC life and outreach. Some church members felt alienated by the rapid changes taking place, the amount of conflict needing to be managed, and how it was being handled. They drifted away to other churches or to no church involvement at all, while a relationally-oriented core hung on.

In this same period, a group of young adults responded to a call I put forth to extend the Reba model into a low-income neighborhood of Chicago. This interracial cluster of communal and congregational members incubated in RPC until they were ready to launch a public worship service in 1995 in nearby Rogers Park. As we became administratively and economically self-sufficient, we became an autonomous Mennonite congregation named Living Water Community Church. RPF accompanied this mission through the purchase of two apartment buildings and a house to facilitate affordable housing and shared proximity, and by loaning money for the purchase of LWCC's own meetinghouse in 2005. RPF now had thirty-two adult members living in two different neighborhoods and worshipping in two separate congregations.

Retooling to welcome a new generation (2000–2010)

In 2002, Reba Place Church called its first non-communal lead pastor. RPC embarked on an extensive consultation process to review its history, discern its unique mission, and more healthfully establish its distinctiveness from RPF. By 2000, the two shrinking communal clusters saw value in coming back together as one and electing one overall leader with term limits. We chose a newer, younger member—a North Park University philosophy professor—to preside over our healing, renewal, and transformation into one group. We took a serious look at the graying of our ranks and the need to create points of entry for young people to experience community as a serious discipleship option. We started a weekly potluck seminar for guests and students to learn about Christian community. We created a summer program and later a nine-month apprenticeship to offer short trial periods of communal life. Under the next elected leader, we created three successive layers of commitment for moving toward covenant membership. We developed a mission statement to help discern and direct our activities: "The calling of RPF is to extend the mission of Jesus by being a community of love and discipleship and by nurturing other such communities as God gives us grace."

I was elected in 2009 as the first woman leader of RPF. With the majority of our forty-three members over sixty-five years old and our oldest member turning ninety, we just welcomed two novices in their late twenties and a young family with two children into covenant membership. Another twenty-nine adults are testing levels of commitment with us. Like Sarah and Abraham, we are giving birth in old age to new community expressions—new households, new businesses—and sharing people and printed resources to help develop new communities.

Reba old-timers identify the greatest challenges of communal living in three primary categories:

- Shared finances and decision-making reveal differences among us which challenge us to listen well to God and to each other.
- Interdependent relationships require us to resolve conflict, give and accept forgiveness, and release hurt.
- Being stretched geographically and with busy lives requires discernment of when we need to say no.

Members name Reba's strengths as clustering around two basic areas.

- What initially drew them: the call to commit to radical discipleship; authentic, heartfelt worship; engaging with the urban context; and an established track record with maturity and wisdom in evidence.
- The fruit coming from long-term participation: navigating conflict and learning from our mistakes; shared economics to accomplish more than we could do on our own; long-term

relational support; and staying-power while experiencing continual transformation over time.

What is leading new and younger people to join RPF and what are the challenges?

Celina Varela shares her story

In the summer of 2006, I traveled from hot and dry Texas to the cooler, more humid Midwest for a visit with Reba Place Fellowship. I had just completed five years in a Baptist seminary with a course that allowed me to travel through India. My journey through the beauty and desolation of that country reminded me of the same trek I took through my biblical studies.

In seminary, I wrestled with the confusing, difficult parts of Scripture, grieved over the ugly parts of church history, and came away still inspired by the wonder of the biblical text and still believing in the power of God's Spirit to act in the midst of a community of people. I was released from the confines of the seminary walls by my professors like a bundle of lavender tossed at a departing newly married couple. There was a hopeful expectation in their parting advice, a belief that I would contribute learned wisdom to any congregation I joined. I left trying to believe I was half as talented as they believed I was.

I took the words of my professors, placed them beside the teachings of Jesus and others who had inspired me, wrapped them up in my handkerchief, tied it to a stick, and set out to find answers to my questions. Of course that wasn't all I had. I had a close group of friends, the support of family, and God's Spirit with me. At the time, though, I felt that these words were my main sources of sustenance. I longed for the kind of faith and church described in their teachings.

So I set out to find a group of people who were living out Jesus' call to peace in a real way. I wanted to be a part of a people who were responding to the words of Jesus in what they did with their money and in how they welcomed the poor. I wanted to see a church community that was living out God's desire to lift the valleys and lower the mountains, making uneven ground level (Isaiah 40:4). I wanted to find a group of people meeting one another's needs in a way that made the distribution even, where no one had more than another. I was specifically hoping to find an intentional Christian community that was intergenerational, in existence for more than ten years, pacifist, and practicing shared finances and resources. My searching brought me to Reba Place Fellowship and I have been a part of this community since then.

My initial participation with RPF began as part of a nine-month program specifically designed to engage young adults who desire to learn more about community living. The program helps newcomers find a way to live within the community without participating fully in practices like the common purse. For many young people, the apprenticeship program provides the clarity and direction needed in navigating the unique aspects of living in an intentional community. With all the unknown that comes with settling into a new place, the apprenticeship program offers ready housing, support for finding a job, and a group of like-minded peers.

It is a credit to Reba Place Fellowship that they continue to provide the resources needed to support newcomers, knowing the financial cost and expecting that while some of the apprentices will stick around, others will eventually move on. The members' commitment to the program is reflective of the persistence and patience shown in other areas of life, contributing to a wisdom and experience that many young people desire to emulate.

During my initial visit to RPF, the experienced wisdom of the members drew me in like an experienced seamstress threading a needle. I wanted to go through the eye of the needle and be guided into the work of God's kingdom among them. RPF members are willing to work with seekers. They are willing to be vulnerable with us, to openly share their mistakes and joys, and eager to be a part of our discipleship process. I was elated to find such a giving community and continue to be blessed in my participation. For someone like me, who learns well through modeling and watching, it was one of the best learning grounds.

Some people who come to RPF are not like me, though. I've grown to appreciate those among us who learn through doing and experimenting on their own. They are the people who readily jump off a diving board because they know the thrill that awaits them. I tend to hang out at the board's edge, thinking through all the things that could go wrong. With visions of bellyflops crashing in my head, I walk down the ladder.

Initially, RPF suits people like me, while those with eager desires to create on their own can experience some of the frustrations that come from being in a settled community. Those with patience to stick around eventually find opportunities to satiate their pioneering spirit. They are the ones starting new households, launching new community projects, and starting new traditions. They discover that RPF is a chameleon community, changing and adapting to meet the needs of its members and in need of risk-takers. For me, having the patience to stick around has resulted in a willingness to move beyond my stance as an observer and to begin asking difficult questions about my involvement with Reba Place Fellowship.

Soon after I came to live in Evanston, I discovered that several members of RPF knew John Howard Yoder as a past friend or colleague. Because his writings were so influential in the formation of my own theological thoughts, I was joyfully surprised; the people I was learning from had rubbed shoulders with John Howard Yoder! Then more surprises came as I learned about his life, including allegations of sexual misconduct that led to a period of church discipline. It was a harsh reminder of the human frailty encountered in our life together and introduced in me a heightened state of curiosity about the history of RPF and the Mennonite faith tradition. The parts of RPF history that are difficult to understand are not regular topics of discussion, nor are they hidden from newcomers. Anyone with enough interest to ask will receive honest reflections about RPF's struggle through the polarized discussion of women in leadership, for example, or about the days of questionable leadership hierarchies.

My experience as a woman at RPF has moments of seeming ease. The southern Baptist world had provided me with a great deal of discipleship and spiritual formation, but it left me with some timidity and uncertainty about leadership in church life. The seminary I attended helped to undo some of the harm and led me on the beginnings of healing from negative thoughts that sprang into my mind every time I had the desire to preach.

As I participate with the community here, I find that my mentors are much like my seminary professors. They are eager to hear about my desires and to encourage abilities they see in me. As a result, I preach at Reba Place Church occasionally. I serve on RPF's current leadership team and was part of the past team in 2008.

When I volunteer to lead our meetings and committees, I am readily received. Our current community leader, Sally, has made great effort to include a number of other women on the leadership team.

Roots that settle are not so easy to dig up, though. The practices embedded by past actions make it difficult to move beyond the historical space where women were not supported in leadership. Historically, RPF never made a concrete decision to keep women out of leadership, but there was enough disagreement on the topic to keep the community from fully affirming the practice. A sparse number of women served on leadership, but most women were happy to serve in other ways.

In 2008, when I served on the leadership team, I was joined by another woman. Many times, I was the only woman present at meetings. I was the note-taker and found it very difficult at times to know how to break into the conversation. I understood, then, the desire by women to serve in other ways. As a recently married person, I find it difficult to break gender roles within our household—and we intentionally try to be mindful about sharing responsibilities in the house. Whenever I find myself going into the kitchen to take over my husband's nights to cook, I lament the immense hold the historical roots of patriarchy have on me.

Beyond the questions that I have about my participation in RPF as a woman, I often find myself wondering about my experience as a Latina. Recent discussions in a group started by Reba Place Church around the topic of racial reconciliation encouraged me to consider my own racial identity formation. As part of that formation, my husband (then fiancé) and I attended a weekend anti-racism training conducted by Crossroads, a group that works to dismantle systemic racism. After the training, I became more aware of the reasons behind my responses to life within the Reba community, which is predominately white. I realized that my difficulty breaking into the discussions around the leadership team circle were not only due to gender roles, but also to my experience as a person of color.

In our anti-racism discussion group, we have agreements for discussion written out on a piece of paper that hangs on the wall. One agreement reads, "Step Up/Step Back." The idea is that those who would normally not speak out agree to comment first and those who are always the first to speak agree to refrain from speaking until others have spoken. Now, whenever I attend RPF meetings, I make that agreement with myself. I force myself to speak out my opinions and ideas, especially when I feel inadequate. I do question how the structures in place at RPF continue to repeat the cycles of racism and desire for new structures to be put in place. Most days, I have no idea how to begin that process, but one good way to start is with discussions identifying unjust structures with the group that formed at Reba following the Crossroads training.

Reba Place Fellowship is far from a perfect community. If I came because I believed it held out to me the practices embodied by the ideals in my head, I did not stay because community living proved to be flawless. I have other questions about being a part of RPF— how do we resist war with our finances? How does RPF's stance as property owners affect our relationships with our neighbors? How do we live in unity while holding different opinions on topics like our acceptance of the LGBT (Gay, Lesbian, Bisexual, and Transgendered) community?

While these questions may affect my decisions regarding whether I join RPF as a full member participating in the common purse, they do not change my desire to be a part of the Reba community. I stay in Evanston because I feel compelled to be a part of this imperfect community. I continue on with this group of people because I believe that no community could possibly be free of all these difficulties. I continue to serve because it is here that I have found people—both within and outside of Reba Place Fellowship—willing to work through the struggle with me. May God give us grace to continue.

CHAPTER FOUR

LEE HEIGHTS COMMUNITY CHURCH: Formed by Diversity

by Regina Shands Stoltzfus

Based on understandings of African American Christianity and African American migration to the north, Regina Shands Stoltzfus offers the story of Lee Heights Community Church. This story, shared through the lens of her personal experience, challenges readers to grapple with what is required in creating interracial congregations. Although not an "intentional Christian community" where members live communally, Lee Heights Community Church is an illuminating example for any Christian community seeking interracial participation and membership.

Formation

I am a product of an Anabaptist denomination's home missions project that planted urban congregations across the Midwest in the mid-twentieth century. The goal of the mission projects was evangelism—reaching out to the lost. In reality, many of the people who came into these churches had a faith tradition already; they were not lost as in "unsaved," but they needed a church home. They also needed a community of faith as a base from which to confront the realities of living within a racist society.

For a research project, I asked my AME (African Methodist Episcopal) raised mother what led her to join the church I was raised and baptized in. I also asked several other women of my mother's generation, women who also had been raised in other denominations, why they chose to attend Mennonite-affiliated churches in the 50s and 60s, when multiracial churches were rare.

I attended this church in urban Ohio all of my childhood and most of my adult life. It is where I formed my Christian identity, where I learned what it means to be part of a worshipping community, and where I learned what most people who go to church don't learn—that multiracial church contexts are possible.

In this place, where my Christian Anabaptist identity was shaped, my African American identity was also nurtured and celebrated. I believe that multiracial church contexts birth generations of people who expect that part of Christian identity is living with people who are not like you racially, culturally, or politically—and yet you choose to be together because you corporately value diversity.

I don't use the word *diversity* to indicate a touchy-feely surface-deep-only colorfulness that looks good on brochures. Instead I suggest an intentional living out of a compelling gospel imperative—the breaking down of walls that divide. These walls are not only about skin color. And the breaking down of walls does not mean simply (and perhaps grudgingly) sharing the same space for a couple of hours each week. It means the intentional coming together of the marginalized and the privileged, a reshaping of an understanding of what it means to be followers of Jesus and members of a church community. It means defying the norms of the larger society.

Each faith community answers questions about identity. Who are we—who shall we be? What will be the defining characteristics of our community? Initially, answers are based on what brought the community together—an agreed upon interpretation of the biblical text, shared theology, and a common understanding of God's call to the community.

Historical and cultural contexts also shape individual and collective identities. Intentionally multiracial faith communities have unique and complicated identities. The increasingly multiracial nature of the United States demands that mono-racial/cultural congregations at least take notice of cultural shifts in cities, towns, and neighborhoods, and learn from the stories of mixed faith communities. I believe faith communities must not only commit themselves to diversity, but also to addressing racist systems and structures, particularly in our own "house." This is the legacy I was given from the church family my mother chose when I was a child.

Historical context

A desire for a new kind of community drove some white Mennonites and African Americans to create multiethnic congregations—a rarity at the dawn of the twenty-first century, but even more so in the 1950s. These experiments were born out of different motives, but established themselves in common desires to live a faith that demonstrated integrity as far as racism and race relations were concerned. They were held together by theologies that affirmed the interconnectness of humanity and called for resistance to the evil of racism and segregation. Differing life experiences and perspectives made the building of these new communities complex. Moreover, it was a sign of radical hospitality on the part of African Americans, relegated by segregation to separate sections of the city, to make a place for white Mennonites among them.

The midpoint of the twentieth century marked a significant convergence of elements that served as catalysts for different ways of imagining community. The first part of the twentieth century saw a huge migration of blacks to the industrial North. Between 1900 and 1910, nearly two hundred thousand African Americans moved north. Failure of cotton crops due to boll weevil infestation rolled across the South, destroying the possibility of work and income for black sharecroppers. By 1914, when World War I broke out, the flow of European immigrants stemmed as demand for U.S. industrial productions were increased. Factories began to recruit blacks from the rural South to keep up with production.

Racial segregation became a marker of northern cities as blacks migrated. In city after city, white families and white-owned institutions colluded with one another to preserve all-white neighborhoods. Violence was not unusual. Although the South often gets painted with a racist brush, the North did more than its share to make sure black people knew their place. Migrants from the South would remark that in the South at least you knew what you were getting with racist white people. In the North, it could come in a more veiled manner, but that did not mean that blacks were not denied housing, employment, etc. In spite of these realities, the opportunity to work was still compelling.

In 1910, Baltimore became the first city to write legislation establishing separate white and black neighborhoods. This legal enforcement followed years of segregation enforced by violence rather than rule of law. It was much more than the simple effect of individual people acting on individual prejudices or of housing patterns being developed by people's preferences to live among their own. The development of segregated neighborhoods involved the collusion of a number of institutions, including mortgage lenders, realtors, neighborhood improvement associations, and local politicians.

By 1930, most cities with significant black populations had established boundaries restricting where blacks could live. This system of segregation was held in place by custom, and later segregation laws were put on the books when migration caused black populations in northern cities to swell.

Neighborhoods changed as white parents pulled their children out of schools where black children began attending. White fears of the increasing black presence got media play, and violence against blacks marked that fear. The machinery of segregation became more sophisticated as restrictive covenants were developed. Contractual agreements among property owners bound them to confirm that they would not sell, lease to, nor allow a black family to occupy the property for a specified period of time, usually ninety-nine years.[1]

By the 1940s, "white Northerners were increasingly justifying segregation, specifically residential segregation, in a very novel way, abandoning claims about racial hierarchy for arguments about the free market for property."[2] The racial hierarchy claims had been dominant in the latter part of the nineteenth and early part of the twentieth century. In terms of housing and economics, the realtor's code, with its "market imperative," complemented arguments about racial incompatibility due to biology.

Riots along the East Coast and throughout the Midwest accelerated the push of black people out of white neighborhoods and helped black neighborhoods become firmly entrenched ghettos by World War II.[3] This was the climate of the country when Mennonites began their urban mission projects in earnest.

African American Christianity

Peter Paris' analysis of the black church's social teachings asserts a doctrine of human equality under God as the final authority for matters of Christian faith, thought, and practice. Correcting the social injustice of racism is considered a moral action in the black church tradition (the seven denominations that are considered the black church, but also black congregations within predominately white denominations). Opposition to racism is a primary factor in the moral code of these churches, most of the time paired with a rejection of violence as an act of justification.[4] The problem of racism is regarded as sin, as a moral failing committed by human beings.

The very origin of black denominations in the United States is grounded in desire for freedom and is oriented toward politicized action and a desire for social change. Black denominations, from their inception, demonstrated the desire of black Christians to be treated with dignity, as human beings, and not to be relegated to second-class citizenry in white churches. This liberation tradition undergirds black Christian ethics. For instance, black womanist ethicist Katie Cannon ("the grandmother of womanist ethics") traces her early shaping of ethics/moral code by pondering the *why* of black people's continued religious devotion in the face of a society that relegated black folks to the bottom of the heap. Her religious wonderings begin with the cognitive dissonance of Christian doctrine and the oppression and exploitation of black people.[5]

The first official Mennonite Church statement addressing racism was released in 1955. At that time, there were 382 African Americans recorded as members and regular attendees in (predominantly white) Mennonite congregations (this figure includes adults, teens, and children).[6]

The middle of the century found white Mennonites moving from isolated farming communities to major cities. As conscientious objectors to war, Mennonite men who otherwise would have been drafted into military service fulfilled their civic duties by entering 1-W service.[7] Common assignments were in hospitals and public service agencies. As the mission agencies set up mission sites around the country, young white men and women participated in voluntary service in African American communities and had their eyes opened to racism and black dissatisfaction with America.

Cannon and others note that African American Christianity is rooted in its African past, as enslaved Africans retained portions of their own religions, and also accepted Christianity—the "white man's religion" and made it their own. Contextualization, reshaping, and recreation formed a significant, important part of the African American religious experience. According to C. Eric Lincoln it was, ". . . something more than a black patina on a white happening. It is a unique response to a historical occurrence that can never be replicated for any people in America."[8]

Historically, the black church in the United States has been the only institution with the ability to be completely controlled by black people. People who attend black Mennonite churches have a double, if not triple consciousness—of being black and being Mennonite.

Those coming from a traditional black church context have the experience of the black church being the center of power within the community. Moreover, black women's experiences are key to understanding the vitality found in the life of the church—a place where there was a sense of being, a sense of having some sort of control.

From Reconstruction, the period of nation-rebuilding following the Civil War, up until the mid-twentieth century, black women were relegated to the sidelines of society in terms of work and livelihood. Only the most menial and poorly paid positions were open to them. It is not surprising within the context of this history that the experience of church being a place of relative power would rub uneasily against an understanding of church that meant one stayed in one's place.

In the context of a church committed to peacemaking, holding an identity formulated on the proposition of being radical for the cause of Christ and the gospel, for being radically committed to an idea of community, and to finding oneself in church congregations planted by pastors and mission workers who didn't mind going against the grain—it is not surprising that these churches would nurture congregants who were not content with a status quo that relegated some members to second class citizenry. My context and the models I had helped me shape what it means to "be church" and work against oppression.

My mother's journey

Born in 1936, my mother, Joyce, was part of the tail end of the African American northern migration stream. Born and raised in Florida, her family members were migrant workers, following the fruit and vegetable crops around the state. Some of the women she knew as a child did domestic work for white families, while others worked as seamstresses for Cypress Gardens, a local tourist attraction. "Fruit and Vacationland, those were our industries," she says.

Joyce came to Cleveland at age twenty-one, in the late fifties, following an uncle and his family, with whom she lived for a while. This was the pattern for many African Americans that migrated; men and women would come one at a time, joining other established family members until they were ready to set out on their own.

Living in the North was a brand new cultural experience. She worked hard to rid herself of her slow southern accent. She saw snow for the first time. She noticed how, on buses, people seemed to not want to talk to one another. Most impressive, however, and most important, was the abundance of jobs. "Jobs, jobs, jobs, for anybody that wanted to work." Good jobs with pensions and insurance benefits.

For women, there were opportunities in shops and factories. As in the South, there were also domestic service jobs. Joyce got a job caring for children, made friends, and developed a social life. Eventually she married another migrant from the South. Her husband, like many other black men in Cleveland, found work in the auto industry. Children followed, and after several years of living in a small inner city apartment, the young couple was able to start thinking about purchasing their own home. A new development was coming up in the southeast tip of the city. Small, basic bungalows were being built, brand new, in a segment of the city that was mostly (and eventually) all black.

With this move, Joyce needed to find a church. She had grown up in the AME church, and during her first years in Cleveland attended the oldest black Baptist church in the city with her extended family members. Now in a new neighborhood, with children of her own, she would be free to make a decision about church on her own, based on her own criteria.

She wanted a neighborhood church—someplace that was accessible and a place that was child-oriented. The Lee Heights church met both of these criteria, and Joyce eventually did a lot of work with the children of that congregation and the surrounding neighborhood. The church's ministries to children and the daycare center housed in the church (owned by another black woman, also a member of the church) allowed Joyce to develop skills that led to her career in child development and care. Joyce said of this community,

"Even though when I first heard about the church I didn't know the basic principles or anything, I just knew it seemed to be a welcoming church that had a lot of faith in the community. The pastors were family oriented and community oriented."

Lee Heights Community Church

Lee Heights Community Church was born out of a Bible fellowship that started in the 1950s and become incorporated as Lee Heights in September 1957. From the beginning, this was an interracial, interdenominational community. The vision of the founding pastors and members was to be grounded in Anabaptist theology, but also not present barriers to people who were seeking church community. This was the reason the name "Mennonite" was never used in the church name. Rather, it was, from the very beginning, a "community" church.

Over the years, the church became a haven for interracial families—this was a safe place for them. During the early years, the bulk of the congregation was composed of people who lived right there in the Lee-Seville community. As second and third generations of Lee Heights folks came along, young people moved out of the neighborhood, but still drove in on Sunday morning.

It was truly a hybrid experience—a new church culture growing out of at least two very distinct streams: African Americans grounded in black church tradition, and Mennonites with roots in Anabaptism going back to the sixteenth century. Together they attempted to live out the creed that was on a sign in the sanctuary: "One in Christ and you are all brothers." The sign in front of the church read, "An Equal Opportunity Faith Family." Even as the neighborhood was experiencing the last vestiges of white flight, black and white members have continued to worship together at Lee Heights for over fifty years. What made such a movement possible?

The community that developed did not seek to avoid or downplay race, culture, or ethnicity. It acknowledged and nurtured black identity and culture while also unapologetically teaching and preaching Anabaptist theology. At times, it was likely an uneasy alliance because of the necessity of sharing power and control. This is the genius of indigenous partnership that J. D. Graber envisioned for the mission churches in the United States. In the 1950s, Graber, then the first general secretary of the Mennonite Board of Missions, called for establishing indigenous churches that would become independent in their own right: a principle that "applies equally to home and foreign, to rural and city missions."[9]

Planting justice

Vincent Harding was the associate pastor at Woodlawn Mennonite Church in Chicago when he and his wife Rosemarie were invited by Mennonite Central Committee's Peace Section to help with a project that was an experiment in promoting peace and reconciliation between blacks and whites. *[For more on the Harding's story, see Chapters 1 and 2.]*

In December, 1961, Rosemarie Harding wrote in a letter to friends:

> What are we doing here, you ask? We have come to Atlanta as Voluntary Servants, under the program of the Mennonite Central Committee—the agency for relief and Christian service of the Mennonite churches. Working with MCC, we have joined a band of several hundred fellow servants. . . We are now searching for ways in which we as individuals, and our churches collectively, can be of help to those persons and groups who are actively seeking reconciliation among men in the South. Thus, the search is really for peace on this section of God's earth—peace, where strife has often been the rule, reconciliation, where mistrust, and fear and prejudice have so long prevailed.[10]

Describing the trip south, she had this to say:

> In North and South Carolina, we told filling station men that we could not use racially segregated toilet facilities, since we, as Christians, did not believe that God intended us to be separated into "Ladies," "Gentlemen," and "Colored." The violence we might have experienced did not come, even though we were occasionally turned aside.[11]

Near the end of the letter:

> We look forward to this experience of life together in Christ, across racial lines, not only because of our particular

backgrounds, but because such persons as Martin Luther King and others have already assured us that our normal life together as Negroes and whites will be the most important aspect of our work in Atlanta.[12]

Rosemarie Harding identified herself as a servant, whose biblical call to witness for peace calls for the defiance of unjust societal conventions and laws.

White church planters and pastors from this era have had the opportunity to reflect upon issues concerning racial identity and church affiliation. From a church history point of view, they have been considered "Urban Pioneers" in multicultural and cross-cultural ministry, providing a necessary role as innovators and teachers. Yet many of them, in retrospect, wished for more guidance and training. Vern and Helen Miller, church planters in Cleveland in the 1950s, when asked, "What supports should the church have been given?" noted they needed training which would have included working with another culture and indigenous church building, while needing less overseeing from the local (established) church and fewer rules regarding church membership.[13]

The Lee Heights church indeed took the "community church" approach seriously and did not require its primarily African American members to identify themselves as Mennonite, although the church is a member of the denomination, and some individuals within the church identify as Mennonite. Most, however, simply identify themselves as Christian. For the African Americans and white people not from a "traditional" Mennonite background, a Mennonite identity is grounded in something outside of theological reflection and more firmly planted in cultural and family history.

However, Mennonite theology and ethics and black church practice coexist in this place, with a specific focus on peacemaking and active work against racism. This church includes as part of its statement of purpose "to establish and maintain a neighborhood church, where among other things, 'people of various denominational backgrounds can find a common meeting ground within the community.'"[14] It seems that here is fertile ground for an expansion of the understanding of Christian identity and community that will be useful for the church as a whole.

The cultural shifts of the twenty-first century present an opportunity to implement lessons we have learned about making space for each other and building new communities. New migration patterns continue to reshape neighborhoods and towns. Fear, distrust, and violence are often the response. Perhaps people of radical faith can present and model new ways of being by understanding our own stories of formation.

CHAPTER FIVE

DISCOVERING THE WAY BY WALKING: An Interview with Hedwig Maria (Hedy) Sawadsky

Conducted by Joanna Shenk

"Go home and work for peace! Stop the refugee crisis from happening. Stop the war." These words spoken to Hedy Sawadsky by a dear Palestinian friend in Jerusalem in 1970 were pivotal for her career. She was serving as a Mennonite Central Committee (MCC) relief worker in Amman, Jordan, and in Jerusalem, with Palestinian refugees. What her friend meant was, "You need to work at the root causes of the violence that create so much suffering for us."

This message is part of Hedy's lifelong work as a peacemaker. "The Palestinian people did me a huge favor in expressing their true feelings. They appreciated our relief work, but were also desperately longing for a peaceful and just life."

Often functioning in behind-the-scenes ways, Hedy Sawadsky supported and continues to support many peacemaking initiatives in Canada and the United States. Now in her eighties, Hedy recently completed twenty-five years of service on the Christian Peacemaker Teams Steering Committee. In this interview, she reflects on her formation, her work with many Christian groups committed to justice, and the importance of divine obedience.

I understand your own family needed to flee from the former Soviet Union. How did that background help set the stage for your work with peacemaking and refugee work?

Oh yes, it was an identification par excellence. My parents were refugees too. Having emigrated in the 1920s, they often expressed their gratitude. Canada contrasted with the hardships, poverty, and lack of freedom in their Ukrainian homeland. For six years our dad was essentially homeless and our mother and her family experienced the shooting of her brother as well as a famine.

One thing that came out of their experience of suffering was a commitment to have their children educated. Their words were, "They can't take that from you." They supported us in our education even though it came at a cost. We were poor. All four of us, my sisters, brother, and I, had the opportunity to attend Christian boarding schools in Ontario. How grateful I am for their sacrifices! It was in my time at boarding school that I made a public commitment to Christ.

Our parents were also deeply respectful of our choices to follow our vocational callings. Their strong Christian faith, as well as their creative, adventuresome spirits surely contributed to this philosophy. From them we learned the virtues of hard work and that life is often a struggle. In the end, both parents lived 102 years. When quizzed about their longevity, the response was "God's grace!"

Having grown up in rural Niagara, then, how did you find your way to the Middle East?

After high school I attended and graduated from Canadian Mennonite Bible College (now Canadian Mennonite University) and then taught in the Rosthern Bible School (Saskatchewan) for several years. I participated in MCC summer voluntary service stints in two Canadian psychiatric hospitals, followed by working with Harvey Taves in the MCC office in Waterloo (Ontario). An inner call then led to a year at Bethel College (Kansas), followed by graduation from Mennonite Biblical Seminary, Elkhart, Indiana. Further discernment led to work in a Mennonite church in Ontario and to teaching in a Mennonite high school.

While working in these church-related settings, I intersected with people who had overseas experience. When I was in my late thirties, the time seemed right to apply for service overseas. Soon I heard from MCC and agreed to go to the Middle East.

So in the summer of 1968, I found myself in Amman, Jordan, a year after the Six Day War between the Israelis and the Palestinians. As a result of the war, hundreds of refugees from places like Jericho and Bethlehem had fled east across the Jordan River and were living in tent camps in Jordan. MCC pioneers, Olga and Harry Martens, had arrived a year earlier and set the stage for a new MCC unit to continue the work.

My responsibilities included training Palestinian women for kindergarten teaching and women's activity centers in the barren camps. Deep respect developed as we MCCers became friends with both refugees and others, the majority of whom were Muslims. Thawabeh, one of these friends, gave me a beautiful Palestinian *fellaheen,* or peasant dress, that she and her mother had made with hand-stitched needlework designs. I still cherish it.

It felt like a gift of God's guidance and grace to be transferred to Jerusalem for my second year in the Middle East. How special to be living in the land where Jesus walked! While working in the MCC needlework shop, I met Palestinians who prepared the needlework, as well as Israelis and visitors from elsewhere. I remember playing the organ for a worship service in the Lutheran Church of the Redeemer! The horizons of my consciousness continued to expand—ecumenically, with the people working in countless NGOs (non-governmental organizations), and as I visited many historical and biblical sites in this land called "Holy."

I also learned to appreciate that there are two sides to the story of conflict between the Israelis and the Palestinians. The imbalance of power seems to be against the Palestinian people who continue to live under occupation. Along with many others, I am hopeful that the deeply longed-for reconciliation will be realized among *all* the "children of Abraham."

And it is from this place that my Palestinian friend courageously issued the call, "Go home, Hedy, and work for peace." I have never forgotten it!

What was it like to return to North America following these formative experiences in the Middle East? What did it look like to work for peace at "home?"

While my consciousness had been raised, I realized that many people in North America saw things differently. Soon after returning to Canada and sharing the Middle East story in my area, I received a call to work at a church in Nebraska. As Christian education director in that large multigenerational Mennonite church, I was able to share my passion for the Middle East. It was a joy to wear my Palestinian dress, show slides, and tell stories of what I had experienced there.

At about the same time, my mind and heart increasingly made connections with the inherent contradiction of praying for peace and paying for war via "war taxes." How could I, as a follower of the Prince of Peace, justify paying for militarism and the building of weapons with my tax dollars? Indeed, these weapons might be used to harm or even kill my friends in the Middle East and people in other places! Increasingly my conscience was bolstered by biblical convictions.

Early on it wasn't evident what to do with this growing awareness. I remember struggling with others who were also trying to find clarity. Later, I worked in a Mennonite church in Pennsylvania where my role included teaching the Sermon on the Mount (Matthew 5–7) to ecumenical women's groups and to young people.

Thus, while living in the state of the Quaker William Penn and delving more deeply into the Scriptures as well as into the sixteenth century Anabaptist witness, the path became clearer. For me the way to go was to live below the war-taxable level.

After considerable discernment, the church's education committee proposed to the church leadership that I would continue in my position but would be paid as a person in Mennonite Voluntary Service, so as to keep my salary under the taxable level. There was some resistance by the church leadership to my becoming a voluntary service worker. Even though there was strong verbal affirmation for our Anabaptist peace position, it was not acceptable to church leadership for me to take this stance and commit to living more simply while still holding the same position.

My resignation meant that I had six months before my two year contract would have been up. I continued wrestling with questions like "How can we, as Mennonites, continue being the quiet in the land when the world is full of violence?"

Where did you go from there?

It so happened that one of the church members needed a ride to Elkhart, Indiana, to attend seminary. Since my car was available, I drove and found myself also taking the Greek summer course with Professor Gertrude Roten. That began a triple focus, lasting three years. First, the "refresher" courses in biblical foundations for peacemaking—it had been fifteen years since my graduation from seminary. Second, my part-time work with Elkhart's poor at Church Community Services. And third, together with others in the Mennonite community, participating in peace ventures at militarized sites. We held vigils and prayed and joined in nonviolent peace witnesses.

Late in 1977, I was preparing to be part of a witness in Washington, D.C. called the "Feast of the Holy Innocents" (Matthew 2). After picking up apples for the trip in Goshen, I had a horrendous accident, being hit by a drunk driver. My car flipped and landed overturned in the middle of rush hour traffic. Miraculously I came out fairly unscathed.

A Mennonite friend who saw the speeding truck prayed for whoever might be hit. I've wondered, did her prayers keep me alive?! It was also amazing that the carload of us who went to D.C. used Marlin Miller's car since mine was totaled. He was the AMBS president at that time. Providing his car was a strong affirmation of our peace witness venture.

As some Mennonites became more involved in nonviolent direct actions for a more peaceful and just planet, debate was also going on among North American Mennonites about being "the quiet in the land," echoing the questions in my own mind. Was nonresistance enough when nuclear weapons were being built and deployed? What did Anabaptists, as a historic peace church, have to say given these realities?

During the time in Elkhart, solid relationships were forged, based on common commitments to more active peacemaking. Retreats and times of contemplation happened as we tried to discern the will of God. Eventually Mary and Peter Sprunger-Froese and I moved to Colorado Springs to be part of a "resistance and assistance" peace community. *[For more on the story of this community, see Chapter 7.]*

We joined with other Mennonites and Catholics, supporting a soup kitchen and a hospitality house in the spirit of the Catholic

Worker. At times we were drawn to divine obedience, in the spirit of the midwives of Exodus 1 and the apostles in Acts 5. These actions, also known as civil disobedience, happened at times at bomb-making plants as well as at other manifestations of the military-industrial complex. Often these actions were preceded and enveloped by prayers, worship, and community-building.

At some point along the pilgrim way, I realized that I resonated deeply with what I read in Jim Douglass' book, *Resistance and Contemplation*. Beginning in the summer of 1993, while living in Amarillo, Texas, I worked closely with Jim and Shelley Douglass for five years as a part of the White Train Campaign, seeking to nonviolently block the shipment of nuclear weapons across the United States.

Surely, the years of action, reading, Bible study, prayer, music making, piano playing, singing, and reveling in the beauty of God's creation, coupled with an array of life experiences and work, have also contributed to this sense of being a "contemplative activist."

How would you describe "contemplative activism" for people who may not understand what that means? What has that meant for you specifically?

The action part, the doing part, is hopefully flowing from the being part of who I am. Worshipping with Quakers in silent meetings, plus going on retreats and fasting, these too have been part of my life. Often I have pondered the significance of the text (Isaiah 43:1-2 NRSV) given to me by my pastor when I was baptized at eighteen. This seems to sum up what we are talking about:

> *Do not fear, for I have redeemed you;*
> *I have called you by name, you are mine.*
> *When you pass through the waters, I will be with you;*
> *and through the rivers, they shall not overwhelm you.*

How do you see Christian Peacemaker Teams embodying the integration of "being" and "doing"? Is it possible for an organization to be oriented in that way?

There were three main points in the original mandate that came out of the Techny (Illinois) meeting, which was the launching point for

Christian Peacemaker Teams (CPT). *[For more on the story of CPT see Chapter 9.]*

1. We believe that the mandate to proclaim the gospel of repentance, salvation, and reconciliation includes a strengthened Biblical peace witness.
2. We believe that faithfulness to what Jesus taught and modeled calls us to more active peacemaking.
3. We believe that a renewed commitment to the gospel of peace calls us to new forms of public witness which may include nonviolent direct action.[1]

Even though it's not stated explicitly, it seems inherent, given the Christ-centeredness of the mandate. Not only did Jesus teach us the importance of prayer and worship, he repeatedly manifested his intimate Oneness with God in his actions and life. Even in the initial training in 1993 the curriculum included corporate worship and contemplative silence times. To my knowledge, all of the training sessions have continued to include daily worship.

Early on, Gene Stoltzfus, the first director of CPT, taught us a prayer song with body motions:

> *Lamb of God, you take away the sins of the world.*
> *Have mercy on us.*
> *Grant us peace.*

We sang it often and in many places; in trainings in North America and even in Iraq during our first overseas delegation in 1990. Clearly, worship and our Christocentric faith have sustained us in the ups and downs of "Being in the Way" nonviolently and often in highly stressful situations.

As someone who grew up in the Canadian context and as a Canadian Mennonite, were there certain perspectives that you felt you were bringing to the U.S. context?

I was a learner, often inspired and challenged by wonderful U.S. friends and coworkers, including Mennonites, Quakers, Catholics, and others.

I recognized I was in the most powerful nation on earth, as they say, and also the most militarized. The urgency of responding as a disciple of Jesus to the violence that was perpetrated by the military-industrial complex was certainly heightened in the United States.

Even now while appreciating my own country, Canada, I also aspire to live respectfully as a global person, especially as climate change is upon us. The song to the tune of "Finlandia" sums this up for me:

This is my song, O God of all the nations
A song of peace, for lands afar and mine
This is my home, the country where my heart is
Here are my hopes, my dreams my holy shrine
But other hearts in other lands are beating
With hopes and dreams as true and high as mine. . .
O hear my song, thou God of all the nations
A song of peace for their land and for mine.

—L. Stone

What about your experience being a woman doing this work?

Early on in my life I was given opportunities. That included MCC assignments beginning in my twenties. In three Mennonite churches, I worked cooperatively with pastors as a Christian education director. In the wider denomination there were leadership postings with Women in Church Vocations and on the General Board of the General Conference Mennonite Church.

At times I did notice that my comments were initially ignored and only taken seriously when restated by a man. This was disappointing and disempowering. Nevertheless, I have learned to trust my intuition and to articulate that awareness more and more.

As a younger woman I am encouraged to hear your story, and it reminds me how important intergenerational relationships are. I know that these types of relationships matter a lot to you.

Over a year ago, a woman in her early twenties walked into my life. I opened my door on a cold and wintry Saturday morning in January, and there she was, walking her cousin's dog. After brief introductions, I invited Deanna in for tea and we chatted. How surprised I was to learn that a friend of hers had recently been on a CPT delegation to Iraq. That is rare in our area, especially if you're from Dutch Reformed Church background. How surprised Deanna was to discover that our friendship would turn out to be the answer to the prayer she had just been praying as she walked the dog!

The friendship deepened as we spent more time together. In the fall of 2010 Deanna continued her adventuresome career and education by following God's call to Canadian Mennonite University in Winnipeg (Man). Then the following winter, about a year after our first amazing divine encounter, she returned for a week of vacation, bringing three friends from CMU with her. They came over to my house for a visit. We drank tea and ate desserts. We made music, laughed, cried, and prayed together. It was a beautiful evening celebrating our common faith and encouraging one another on the journey.

The cloud of witnesses surrounding us draws us to overcome the barriers, such as ageism and racism that could divide us, and find a place where we can sit together, rejoice, and learn from one another.

These vibrant young women represent the best in your generation, Joanna, as they aspire to walk in the Way of Jesus. As one who grew up in an earlier time, I lament the mess we've made of God's exquisite creation. May my peers and I support you with our prayers and love. You inspire hope that as "my life flows on in endless song, above earth's lamentation, I catch the sweet, though far off hymn that hails a new creation" (R. Lowry).

I don't have daughters and sons of my own. Nevertheless, I feel graced to have divine encounters of a different sort and receive blessings a hundredfold (Matthew 19:29).

What a beautiful understanding of family. As a daughter, when you reflect on your relationship with your parents, what was it like caring for them in their later years and continuing your work as a peacemaker in various capacities?

Herman and Anna Berg Sawadsky are now in their heavenly home. Their voices are quiet, their spirits echo still.

After living in the United States over twenty years, although not consecutively, I returned home to Ontario to be closer to my aging parents, who were nearing ninety. This move too felt like a call from God. Work with CPT continued, overlapping with peace and justice ministries with MCC Ontario. Extensive traveling meant that I was often away for weeks at a time.

Whenever I returned to Vineland, I would find lovely notes and cards, signed by my parents saying, "We love you, we missed you, we're so glad you're back." An especially precious memory lingers. My dad, at one hundred years old, had become legally blind. On a sheet of paper he had written in big capital letters, "<u>LIEBE HEDY</u>! HERZLICH WILLKOMEN ALS FRIEDENS STIFTER! LOVE: MAMA & PAPA" (Welcome home, peacemaker! Mom and Dad).

Over the years my parents had graciously supported, but not always understood, the pathway of their oldest daughter. This unexpected affirmation from my parents moved my heart beyond all expectations. The "go home and work for peace" of half a lifetime ago had somehow come full circle.

> "Glory to God in the highest heaven, and on earth peace among those whom he favors!"
> —Luke 2:14 NRSV

Part Two

SECOND WAVE
(1970s *and* 80s)

CHAPTER SIX

SHAPED BY SOJOURNERS:
Choosing the Heat

By André Gingerich Stoner

As a young adult Mennonite, André Gingerich Stoner chose to take a year off college in 1981–82 and volunteer with the Sojourners community in Washington, D.C. During that year he was inspired and challenged by Sojourners' communal living and commitment to peacemaking in a low-income neighborhood of D.C. What he had learned in theory from the Mennonite tradition, he saw lived out in the context of this ecumenical community.

It was August of 1982 and I was driving my parents' old Audi down Interstate 81, back to Harrisonburg, Virginia, where I would spend a few days before taking off for my junior year of college. I was just coming from a three day silent retreat at the end of a voluntary service year with the Sojourners community in Washington, D.C. It had been quite a year and I was trying to make sense of it.

I remembered how I had gotten to D.C. and Sojourners. I was studying at Swarthmore College, a small school in Pennsylvania with strong academics and many affluent and privileged students. I had come to D.C. to spend the weekend with my friend Luke and to work together on a newsletter for Mennonite non-registrants. Luke wanted to introduce me to Phil Baker-Shenk, a Mennonite several years older than we were, who had edited a collection of stories of Vietnam-era draft resisters.

Phil was worshipping with the Sojourners community. I didn't know much about them, but my parents subscribed to their magazine and it was on the shelves of the library at Eastern Mennonite High School. I remember picking up an issue while I was a high school student that contained articles by several Mennonites including Willard Swartley, the father of a good friend of mine, and John Stoner, who worked at the Mennonite Central Committee (little did I know he would become my father-in-law).

Luke and I met Phil at Millie and Al's, a pizza joint on Eighteenth Street in the Adams Morgan neighborhood. We talked about registration and draft resistance. Then I told them about how hard it was for me to find my place at Swarthmore. There were lots of folks who cared about peace and social justice, usually in a Kennedy-liberal kind of way. But there was hardly anyone who understood or spoke a faith language, much less in a way that connected Jesus to the needs of the world around us.

In the Quaker meeting I was more likely to hear a poem by Robert Frost than a saying of Jesus. For a while I took the train and a bus into Philly to worship at Diamond Street Mennonite Church, but that was another foreign world. At some point, Phil said, "You should come spend a year working and worshipping with the Sojourners community."

I think it was the next day that he and I stopped in on Jim Wallis watching a football game in one of the community's group houses on Thirteenth Street. Phil introduced me and we tested the idea. Phil said he'd help me connect with the Mennonite Voluntary Service program that had a house a few blocks away, if I could work at Sojourners. Within a couple of weeks everything was in place.

After a summer bagging groceries at Red Front Supermarket in Harrisonburg, I was off for D.C. I lived in a big house with three or four other Mennonite volunteers and again as many renters. Group life was pretty low-key. We usually ate supper together and would have a house meeting once a week. We worshipped at different churches around town.

Work at the Southern Columbia Heights Tenants Union (otherwise known as the Sojourners Housing Ministry) was anything but low-key. At first I answered phones and tagged along to meetings, but before long I was knocking on doors and getting to know my neighbors, especially folks living in large apartment buildings.

After a brief introduction, I would ask them if they were having any trouble with their landlords, and soon I'd hear a litany of woes. I spent lots of time at one large apartment building with fifty-two units. Tenants would take me into their apartments and show me peeling paint, loose windows, and plaster that had fallen because of leaking pipes. In the winter, time and again, the hot water would fail and the heat would be off. And this was just one building in one neighborhood in one of many cities in our country. I had had no idea of these kinds of conditions.

Over time I got to know the tenants. An older woman who worked at a factory seemed to be a natural leader. There was a young mother with three kids at home and a student from the Caribbean. There were also several Salvadoran families. I would stop by nearly every day and sit in living rooms or on the front steps, talking and listening. Finally someone said they'd invite other tenants to their apartment to talk about what they could do together. No one thought anybody else would come. But they did, and so we met and planned.

We scheduled housing inspections and then went down to the Housing Department to insist that inspectors followed up on the inspections. I discovered that the inspectors would not return calls from tenants who lived and suffered in the building, but my nineteen-year-old white, male voice got a quick response. That was a lesson about race and privilege that I have never forgotten.

We did research on who owned the building and met with the property manager. The first time we met in his Maryland office. He sat behind a big desk and we sat in little folding chairs. The next time we met in one of the apartments and he sat in a chair in the middle of the room. Sometimes we invited the television station. Together we learned about the difference between a power that intimidates and controls, and the power of numbers that holds someone accountable. As my new friends pulled together, the pipes got fixed and the heat got turned on. Every once in a while, they would get together with tenants from other buildings to testify at a city council meeting. This was like no education I had gotten in college.

My mentors and trainers were members of the Sojourners community. They lived together in half a dozen houses in the neighborhood. Most had come from white middle-class families. Some had given up lucrative jobs and promising career tracks to eat rice and lentils and get a couple of dollars a month as spending money. There were a few Mennonites in the mix—it was somewhat comforting to me to meet Benders and Brubakers and Longeneckers. Others were evangelicals or Methodists or Catholics—and those labels didn't seem to make any difference. Here, people lived out their faith. They were talking about Jesus and they were following Jesus. In my Mennonite church growing up, I had heard people talk about simple living, but these people were *doing* it. Growing up I had heard people talk about community, but these people were trying it out. These folks were serving the poor, but even more, they were becoming friends with their neighbors. And most of the time, they seemed to be having fun.

Early on, I started worshipping with the Sojourners community on Sunday nights. It was an intriguing combination of casual and informal worship among friends, yet followed an almost liturgical order. Here was a chance to hear folks reflect on Scripture out of this experience of following Jesus each day in the heart of the city. People shared testimonies and prayer concerns. There was a richness about worship with people who shared their daily life together. I came to really value the weekly communion service, ritually done each week in the same way with the same songs. And each week full with new meaning.

In the spring, I was asked to speak on *The Today Show* about my choice not to register for the draft. It was a heady and scary moment. I knew I faced a possible five-year jail term. I had considerable support, so I decided to go ahead. The interview was on a Monday morning. The night before, during regular Sojourners worship, the worship leader asked if they could pray for me. I said yes, of course.

They asked me to come forward and everyone gathered around me to lay hands on me. This was nothing I had experienced before. I have no idea what words were spoken, but I remember looking around and thinking, "I'm not taking this risk alone." All these people had taken similar risks in their own lives. They'd made choices for God's kingdom that had a cost. They were backing me up with their lives. And I knew these people loved me. As they put their hands on my shoulders and head, I felt a warmth that I had not known before. Only later did I find the words—that was God's love and grace.

And of course, I read the magazine that other members of the community wrote, edited, and published. The articles gave me ways to think about the events of our neighborhood and our world. They connected the biblical story with my own experiences. Sometimes there were articles by Mennonites, but usually the magazine introduced me to Christians from many places living out their faith in radical ways.

In working, watching, eating, reading, and worshipping with folks from Sojourners, I would often find myself thinking: these folks are actually living out their faith the way my Mennonite church told me we were supposed to do it.

I was often surprised at how small the group was, how ordinary many of the members were, and how great an impact they had on their community and the broader world.

So after a year in D.C., I was pondering all these things on that car ride down I-81 through the Shenandoah Valley on my way to Harrisonburg. Someone at Sojourners had given me the address for a Jesuit retreat center. Spending three days in silence was a strange and scary thing for me, but it seemed to be important to these people I had been with for the year, so I thought I'd give it a try. I thought back over the year and journaled about it. I was thinking about my future back in college. I think I was hoping for a big insight. It never came.

It was a sweltering Virginia day as I drove. I had the windows rolled all the way down, the air was rushing past me, and still I was sweating. I looked up and a car was passing me with the windows rolled up tight. Strange, I thought, don't they know it's hot out here? Then I realized they must have air conditioning (those were the days before every car had air conditioning).

Then suddenly it struck me: for nearly twenty years I had been living in air-conditioned comfort and I had had no idea that it was hot as hell outside. But during this year, I found out. Then I asked myself, where would Jesus be? And I knew Jesus would be out in the streets where it was hot. At that moment it became clear to me that though I might enjoy a little air conditioning from time to time, if I wanted to be with Jesus, I would spend most of my life out in the streets where it was hot.

As I look back, I can see that during that year in the early 80s with Sojourners, many seeds were planted which later took root in my life. From then on I have lived in or at the edge of alternative Christian communities. For three years after college I worked

with Church and Peace, a European network of intentional communities and congregations that shared a peace church vision. I shared
an office and daily prayers with members of the Laurentiuskonvent,
a community growing out of experiences of the Confessing Church.[1]
During that time I visited and became friends with many of the communities in the Church and Peace network, from Protestant monastic
communities devoted to a life of prayer, to worker priest communities, to a Mennonite house fellowship, and a group that I would best
describe as a Hutterite Catholic Worker community!

I became friends with several German couples in that network,
and the five of us formed a community and lived together for
three years as part of a peace witness just a mile from a large U.S.
nuclear weapons base. During this time Cathy and I got married,
and we worked together in building relationships with U.S. military personnel in the region.

When we returned to the United States, a group of Mennonite
intentional neighbors in Lancaster, Pennsylvania, invited us to live
in an apartment they had while we got our feet on the ground. We
received support and encouragement as a young couple during a
critical time in our marriage. Later, while in seminary at Associated
Mennonite Biblical Seminary, we were part of the Fellowship of
Hope church in Elkhart, Indiana, which had earlier been part of the
Shalom Communities Network.

In all these settings we have discovered the joys as well as the
challenges of communal life. But after my year at Sojourners, I could
no longer imagine life just as a nuclear family with a TV and a two-
car garage. I also couldn't imagine getting a job just to make money.
At Sojourners, and along the way, I had met people who lived on
very little and I discovered I could do that too. I also discovered the
exhilaration of doing something that was meaningful and challenging—whether it paid or not. At the end of 2011, at age forty-eight,
for the first time in my life, I have a full-time paying job.

I'm sure that the experience with Sojourners shaped the choices
Cathy and I have made to live in low-income neighborhoods—not
so much because we thought we could make a grand difference,
but because we wanted to remember that it was hot outside and
because we wanted to be with Jesus. And that experience taught
me that the most powerful way for Christians to impact the world
around them is not to go to Capitol Hill, but to gather around

Jesus and to share life together that is radically shaped and guided by him.

For the last number of years, Cathy and I have lived as intentional neighbors with three other households in South Bend, Indiana. We share cars, washing machines, child care, guitar lessons, and eggs. We have separate finances but we give each other "refrigerator rights." We pray together, listen to each other's struggles, and help each other sort through big decisions.

We are in our twenties, forties, and sixties. We are single and married, with and without kids. Some of us are part of Kern Road Mennonite Church. Together we host a community meal twice a month for friends and neighbors who gather to break bread with each other. Our mortgage is cheap enough and our cars old enough that we have been able to live very well on a modest income allowing one of us to be home full-time with our children and neighbors. We live in a neighborhood that constantly reminds us of the divisions of race in our culture and the wounds of poverty. But we catch glimpses of the kingdom in conversations with neighbor kids who come to play basketball or pump up their bike tires. Or when another neighbor drops in to teach us how to fry okra or the ninety-two-year-old woman from across the street (who we now visit in a nursing home) tells us she loves us.

Since my experience in D.C., Sojourners has changed significantly. It is no longer an intentional community. In quite a different way, it continues to challenge and encourage Christians to live a Jesus-centered life. But still, new communities and fresh expressions of church are emerging all around us.

Many Christians are rediscovering living in community, sharing life with the poor, and seeking to love even their enemies. Even though we may think of these as uniquely Mennonite concerns, we Mennonites didn't make this stuff up. We shouldn't be surprised that whenever people read the Bible and try to take Jesus seriously, they come to this place. Sometimes these discipleship-oriented Christians have taken inspiration from Mennonites and the Anabaptist tradition, but often they live out the gospel far more radically than Mennonites do.

After five hundred years, those of us who are Mennonite have traditions and institutions and resources that enrich us, but we've also become quite comfortable in the land of the "brave and the free" even as we carry historical baggage and cultural trappings that weigh us down. So those with a five-hundred-year tradition and those discovering the joy of discipleship in new ways, the old and the new Anabaptists, the geriatric peace churches and the new peace churches—we have a lot that we can learn from each other and give each other as we seek to follow Jesus today. It is my hope and prayer that we will continue to challenge and encourage each other as we find ways to walk together.

CHAPTER SEVEN

BIJOU STREET COMMUNITY:
Anabaptists in Babylon

By Mary and Peter Sprunger-Froese

Since 1979 Mary and Peter Sprunger-Froese have lived in Colorado Springs, Colorado, as a part of an ecumenical Christian community committed to peacemaking. This city, known more recently as a hub for evangelical Christian organizations such as Focus on the Family, Navigators, and Compassion International, is also home to five military bases. From this context, Mary and Peter reflect on their experience as Anabaptist Christians, offering perspectives and questions to the broader church.

In November of 1978, we embarked on a community journey. Now, thirty-three years later, we continue loving, learning, persisting, and resisting with a faith-based intentional community in Colorado Springs. Sometimes frayed and afraid, sometimes hopeful and determined, we give thanks for a Christian base in this military Mecca. We long for more—for churches, congregations who will walk with us, with whom we can struggle, support, discern, and serve—in a city immersed in American patriotism, ringed by five military bases, wrought with military assumptions and institutions. Local churches and parachurch organizations fill eight pages in our phone book. Almost unanimously, they support and even encourage this military reality. We long for the light and witness of a body that reconciles all things in Christ, that redeems those left out, and that resists "Caesar" and his empire.

Newly married, we visited Colorado Springs that November of 1978. We were to connect with our friend Hedy Sawadsky. *[For more on Hedy's story, read Chapter 5.]* We had met during our studies at Associated Mennonite Biblical Seminaries (AMBS) in Elkhart, Indiana, and decided together that our paths would join in a search for Christian community that worked with the poor and embraced peacemaking.

While exploring a Voluntary Service (VS) position, we three attended a meeting preparing for an Advent peace vigil at the Air Force Academy. A Mennonite couple at this meeting, Larry and Laurie Hesed, invited us to visit their community the following day. The VS option offered only one position for two years. We were ready for long-term commitment, so we decided to meet with the Heseds and the Catholic couple with whom they lived and worked, Steve Handen and Mary Lynn Sheetz, with baby Emmy.

For several hours we heard about the Weber Street community. The two couples ran a soup kitchen and a hospitality house for homeless folks, while actively protesting war and praying for peace. They drew inspiration from the Catholic Worker movement— communities following the example of Dorothy Day and Peter Maurin, Catholic pacifists who lived among the poor while advocating and agitating for a "new society within the shell of the old."

Steve and Mary Lynn had supported conscientious objectors during the Vietnam War. Steve was a former priest who'd lost his credentials because of the backlash from his anti-war efforts while serving a congregation with many military members—the norm in Colorado Springs, we were to discover. The community sought to bring a peace witness in many forms. Steve and Mary Lynn attended a Catholic parish, and Larry and Laurie were members of a Mennonite church. They made it clear that this was a community of "work," not a church. A common understanding of the gospel was a base for their vision and work. Church participation could be chosen as each person willed.

The community had a common purse of shared money and resources, and community members had part-time paying work to support themselves and live under the taxable level, as war tax resisters and advocates of simple living. By the end of the meeting, it "seemed good to the Holy Spirit and to us" to join this little community. Hedy returned to Elkhart to tie up loose ends, and we returned to Canada where Peter got documents for the move to the United States. We felt led and called.

Colorado beginnings—from Mary

When we got off the bus in Colorado Springs in March of 1979, a woman named Donna picked us up. We went straight to the Weber House, where she and Mary Lynn were ink-deep into silkscreening posters that said "Close Rocky Flats" (the bomb factory near Denver). We discovered the community was now more than twice its November size; a Franciscan nun, a Methodist, and a Catholic woman had also joined. Donna, who lived separately, was also part of the Weber Street community.

The next day—three days after the Three Mile Island nuclear reactor meltdown (March 28, 1979)—we passed out anti-nuclear flyers to movie-goers at the theater showing *The China Syndrome,* a fictional film about nuclear meltdown. The following week, Holy Week, we fasted. I had never fasted—and this was the week of our first wedding anniversary! I was beginning to think we were experiencing a baptism by fire.

The next few years, our community continued hospitality work with homeless people, soup kitchen duty, peace vigils, demonstrations, speaker events, visits to congressional offices, and line-crossings at military bases. We had weekly morning meetings about how to work with residents of the hospitality house and weekly Saturday night meetings about everything else. We also visited one of the local Mennonite churches for a few years.

Quite involved in the Rocky Flats protests that engaged hundreds of people over several years, many of us were arrested and did jail time. We also entered local army and air force bases, sometimes with leaflets, sometimes with simple prayers. Once we took a solar oven and gardening tools to begin a swords-to-plowshares conversion on an air force base. Another time we attempted a citizen's arrest with a warrant for the base commander for war crimes.

These actions sprang from our life together and our understanding of the need to resist the way of death so profitable for the few and so destructive to the many. Prayer times and "discerning" meetings preceded these events. Friends joined us, whether challenging the law or offering food, prayers, calls, and visits. But never did a congregation participate in these events or offer support. Was that because we didn't regularly participate in congregational life? Was our community perceived as exclusive?

Changes in community life—from Mary

In 1981, the Weber Street community became the Bijou community when we moved the hospitality house to Bijou Street. With donations from many supporters, we formed a land trust—a legal entity that holds and protects land for a specific purpose—so that Bijou House could remain "in trust" for low-income people, never to be sold for profit or speculation. Ithaka Land Trust grew, and today it houses many families and single persons and is managed by leaders outside the community.

The communal purse transitioned to individual finances, as finding work and continuing war tax resistance took different forms. Always, donations were designated for the Bijou House or soup kitchen. We supported ourselves with part-time work, though of course subsidized by low-income rent from the land trust and donated food from several stores. We also benefited from a sliding-scale health center, begun by Steve and a few friends.

Community members came and went. Hedy moved to host a peace house in Texas next to a nuclear weapons plant. Larry and Laurie moved to a Kansas farm, making community with Dominican Sisters. Esther Kisamore, a Mennonite who was part of the Bridge Street household in Goshen with me [which also included James Nelson Gingerich, who shares in Chapter 10], came to join us. Many young people came via a local college—sometimes cooking one night a week at Bijou House, sometimes gardening, sometimes acting with my theater troupe, sometimes living with us and staying months or years. Social services students from Sweden came for a year abroad and worked at Bijou House. Volunteers from a Catholic project came for stints from several weeks to several months.

"The Bijou community" came to mean anyone who identified with that name. We agreed that community takes many forms. Many people were a part of community life and work—some focusing on hospitality, some participating in peace events, some planning barbecues and ballgames, and some filling in as needs arose.

Community projects expanded as more volunteers chose ways to participate. Mary Lynn and Donna formed Alterni-Tees, a T-shirt design effort, making shirts with a message—and proceeds went back into projects the shirts supported. Bill initiated CPIS, Citizens for Peace in Space, a group researching and acting against U.S. militarization of space. Peter began a free bike clinic for indigent folks. He discovered many peace and justice teaching opportunities with clients and interested visiting school and church groups. He designed solar ovens and customized them repeatedly. Esther coordinated a personal nonviolence program with the local justice and peace commission. I directed First Strike Theatre, a social justice and nonviolence troupe that created full-length shows as well as street theater, also partnered with the local justice and peace commission.

On July 4, 1993, Esther, Peter, and I began a Sunday school in our home. It seemed the perfect day to begin this intentional gathering together under Jesus' lordship. We had felt church membership was not practical or possible; having no car, transportation to a Mennonite church presented a significant challenge when our community commitments took so much of our time and life. So how could we accountably be part of a congregation if all we could contribute was Sunday morning attendance? That's not Anabaptist at all!

Thus we began the Sunday school experiment as a prayer for guidance in following Jesus. The prayer continues today, though our gathering remains small. We enjoy ongoing informal relationships with local Mennonites and appreciate times when our ministries and worship overlap.

In 1995, the community turned the soup kitchen over to a local nonprofit. Numbers of people eating at the kitchen had burgeoned, and local food banks pressured us for paperwork and nonprofit status. Always volunteer-based and low-key, our "management style" didn't mesh with some of the donor requirements. Today the soup kitchen still serves people and is run by employees of the nonprofit.

In 2006, we closed Bijou House. The 24-7 supervision needed for this home of twelve to fourteen people—mentally ill, addicted, recently prison-released—was too demanding for our small force of aging volunteers. Making the decision was difficult and took time, as we reckoned with the hub that the house had been for attracting so many people—volunteers, friends, community. The land trust took over managing the Bijou House, which now required less supervision because residents were more self-sufficient.

Since then, members of the Bijou community still volunteer at several homes of hospitality—cooking, visiting, and organizing medications. These homes are run by the land trust or live-in hosts. At the columbarium, a memorial garden behind Bijou House, we still hold memorial services for folks who have died homeless or who worked with the homeless.

Peter continues his own bike clinic. A new one, Bike Clinic Too, has also been operating for just over a year; here, another mechanic offers free bikes and friendship to folks this society deems expendable. First Strike Theatre ended its run in 2002 when core members left for new horizons and funding seemed impossible. I began teaching part-time ESOL (English for speakers of other languages) in the public school system and continue in that work. I also create theatrical forays alone or with others whenever possible.

Bijou's work is mortal. The church's mission is not. Our community's work has changed over the years according to the people and energies present. We continue to invite and welcome anyone interested in joining us, however briefly or long-term. While our little ecumenical community may die along with us, we trust God's re-birthing of the church in many forms.

Further observations from Colorado Springs—from Peter

• Since the mid-eighties, local church-sponsored service agencies have increased in number and programs. Bijou and local Mennonites participate in these efforts. While many service providers note inadequacies in government provisions, most continue a basic trust in the U.S. system—implicitly or explicitly—especially when it comes to international conflict.

This blend of systemic trust with quite altruistic social service can be puzzling. An *apoliticized* theology (that is, status-quo politics) is largely to blame and rarely recognized. And what about social psychology? To hand out the proverbial "bowl of soup" to a hungry, grateful person is meaningful to the giver. Is cultural critique even possible when "feel good" assistance work is so singularly honored and identity is defined first in the nation-state rather than in the church? Have Mennonites, in their service orientation, also accommodated to the culture rather than defining dissent as an essential service we can offer?

• Just prior to the Gulf War (1990–91), Bijou gratefully participated in a five hundred-person prayer meeting at the diocesan cathedral, prepared weeks prior by a multidenominational committee. The next day, George Bush Sr. launched the war. Despite their resolute prayer concern for peace the day before, attendees from the prayer service now defended the "necessity" of the war. One of the participating prayer service congregations suddenly changed their no-flag decorum to a pervasive U.S. flag presence throughout their building and at their entrance.

• Former President George W. Bush's "born-again" testimony has been theologically consoling to most Colorado Springs churches and was reason to support the war he initiated. Ignoring this disconnect between faith and life is deeply inconsistent with Judeo-Christian teaching. Maybe this is a reason for the increasing notion among young and old: Jesus? Yes! Christianity? No!

• For eight years, a Catholic sister in the Bijou community has led and pushed for an annual "Sisters Witness against War" event near Hiroshima Day. Catholic sisters from the area participate in a lunch, entertainment, a prayer service, and a vigil at Peterson Air Force Base. As leaders in their church, they want to call Catholics to resist war-making in the Spirit of the Prince of Peace. What could an Anabaptist equivalent be?

• In 2003 several agnostic friends shared their postmodern logic against various traditional arguments for the existence of God. We pondered the impossibility of an objective starting point for any universal truth claims. All of us decried the United States' "freewheeling" military might in the Middle East. The agnostics' cynicism indicted the extensive history of U.S. imperialism. We suggested the impossibility of any clean break with the war culture, noting the complicity of anyone who purchases fossil fuel.

We agreed that all social change begins at the bottom. We then asked how grassroots potential could be tapped. Silence. So we followed up with another question: What would you do if you encountered a church that at its core—in word and deed—was resolutely against the war culture's most overt features (i.e. personnel, money, ideology, scientific and technological support)? These agnostics' prompt response: "We'd break down the doors of such a church to get in!"

• Presbyterian volunteers teach, visit with, and welcome the adult refugees in Mary's English class. Their church offers the space free of charge for the classes. These volunteers take ministry seriously and are wholeheartedly committed to the beginning students.

One offers an after-class field trip to the Iranian family, Christians who were persecuted in their home country. She and her husband take the family to the Air Force Academy to see the fighter jets—their son wants to be a pilot. Another volunteer goes to USO dances (the national nonprofit that supports the troops and their families) on the weekend. One volunteer leaves for special secret duty with a contractor in Afghanistan. Most volunteers have some relationship to the Air Force. The teacher for the intermediate class taught ESL for NATO in Europe—her husband is retired from the Air Force.

In after-class conversations, several have learned Mary is a Mennonite. To date, there has been no response to this identity. How we wish our church could be so visibly making peace and resisting Caesar that these volunteers would exclaim, "Oh! *That church?!*"

Living as Anabaptists in Babylon

Since I, Peter, was eighteen, thanks to parental example and an Old Colony Mennonite background, I identified myself and those committed to the church as resident aliens. Two years at AMBS confirmed and deepened this conviction. Seminary teaching reinforced the power of the church against the tribal god of the nation-state. This learning was a "treasure in earthen vessels" (2 Corinthians 4:7) for a world starved for an Anabaptist perspective.

Following her parents' example of active participation in the Berne (Indiana) Mennonite church, Mary found church life core to her faith. Intentional households after college challenged her understandings of U.S. policies and initiated her into war tax resistance. Study at AMBS introduced her to me and to Hedy, whose talk of "divine obedience" that sometimes countered human laws scared her. And then in a Pentateuch class, Professor Millard Lind made it clear that the Shema ("Hear O Israel. . .The Lord is one. . ."

Deuteronomy 4:6) was Israel's worship—its pledge of allegiance. Lind's "worship is a political act" capsized a boatload of fears about the risks in "obeying God rather than (hu)man." Millard was talking about faithfulness—this was biblical!

Living in militarized Colorado Springs convinces us that all North Americans live in Babylon. Recent celebrative reactions to Osama Bin Laden's death are a stunning example. The Empire's reach includes church sanction, social approval, school partnerships, and commercial investment and profit.

Every day we feel our alien status: we are pilgrims and strangers in this American city. Sometimes tempted to see our role as hospice workers—attending a dying planet with compassion and acceptance—we nevertheless find the compelling Anabaptist witness a life-giving hope. What a light Anabaptists have to offer! Amish forgiveness of the Nickel Mines school shootings burst Christ's love around the world. What other examples of body witness can we ignite?

Peace activism has garnered praise as a "special calling on behalf of the world." The "universal lordship of Christ" theme has reached beyond traditional alternatives for draft-age youth and has become core to Mennonite activists as they "hit the streets" or seek to intervene in conflicted hotbeds. *[For more about this, read about Christian Peacemaker Teams in Chapter 9.]* Still, we're concerned about how Anabaptist-Mennonite ecclesiology might address the individual activist peace-waging model.

When peace-waging is understood first as *individual protest activity*, it becomes a repeat-project seeking to educate and amass ever-larger crowds of effective dissent against the dominating system. As such, it lacks the potential power of church-as-body dissent. Despite the overlap in these two paradigms, the difference is noteworthy. Prior to and more basic than the sum total of individual protest, the church's dissent is as a *minority society within larger society*. In the biblical-Anabaptist sense, this is "being in the world but not of it." The body of Christ resists and builds with kin(g)dom values, hatched and embedded through intergenerational teaching, spirit-building, and identity-formation. Its members, being *body* before *individuals*, are voluntarily committed to *their* society's values.

Congregations living simply, initiating and participating en masse in public protest activity, welcoming outsiders (homeless, undocumented, homosexual, conscience-stricken soldiers, or military contractors), or creating war-tax-resistance discernment circles—these are examples of body protest. When we Mennonites become known for our unwavering allegiance to the untamed counter-society of Jesus, sharing our Mennonite roots with patriotic believers will break ground for new ecumenical witness to the reconciling power of Christ. We need and long for this witness. May we be part of God's ongoing revolutionary tap-on-the-shoulder.

CHAPTER EIGHT

LIFE IN COMMUNITY:
An Illustrated Journey

By Dawn Longenecker with illustrations by Sam Jerome

Through word and image, follow Dawn Longenecker's journey with various Christian communities. Shaped in the Mennonite tradition as a peacemaker, Dawn did not always choose to stay within Mennonite church contexts. Her story illustrates that participation in intentional community can be a lifelong commitment, whether married or unmarried, with or without children. She challenges readers to take seriously Jesus' call to seek justice and work for reconciliation, no matter their church context.

I grew up in the Mennonite Church. At Lebanon Mennonite Church (Lebanon, Oregon), my father, Dan, was the pastor and a Sunday school teacher. I remember he shared his story of serving in 1-W service as a young man instead of serving in the military. This had a powerful impact on me as I thought about my own call to be a peacemaker.

At Line Lexington Mennonite Church (Lexington, Pennsylvania) where my Dad also pastored, I remember that the youth pastor assisted all young people in writing our own conscientious

---

All the illustration credits in this chapter belong to Sam Jerome. The Eastern Mennonite College logo is adapted with permission from Eastern Mennonite University.

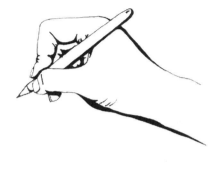

objector statements. Even though I'm female and didn't have to worry that I might be drafted, it was explained to me that this was an important process for every member of the Mennonite Church. I still believe this to be true.

Going to Eastern Mennonite University (then College) was a deepening experience. There I was challenged to think about peacemaking as "active" and not "passive." This understanding drew me to the Sojourners Community and their active peacemaking and public worship witnesses in my post-college days.

My sophomore year in college was spent in Washington, D.C., through the Washington Study Service Year program sponsored by Eastern Mennonite College (the program has been renamed "Washington Scholars Program" in recent years).

I was learning about social justice and the need for Christians to hold institutions and government accountable to serve humanity and live up to the principles of justice and peace for all people. We were taught to hold in tension the value of institutions, which are needed in society, with the recognition that institutions can become tools for those in power to promote and maintain a status quo, which often works against justice for the poor.

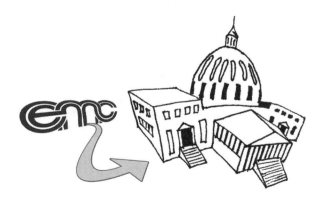

That was the year 1977–78 and a radical Christian group in D.C. called the Community for Creative Non-Violence (CCNV) was active in fighting for the rights of homeless people.

Mitch Snyder, their leader, who had previously been homeless and incarcerated for theft, became an effective advocate for this cause. He was converted to Christianity by the Berrigan brothers, peace activists who spent time in jail with him.

Mitch learned that nonviolent acts of civil disobedience can be used to confront institutions that are not honoring people's basic rights. Once Mitch led CCNV in serving a meal to senators and

Mitch Snyder, activist with the Community for Creative Non-Violence.

members of Congress on the downtown mall with food salvaged from dumpsters to show how much food gets wasted while people go hungry.

CCNV put out a call to area churches to open their doors to the homeless during a time when urban homelessness was at a

Brothers Daniel and Philip Berrigan, nonviolent Christian activists, became well known to the public in the 1960s when they burned draft cards in protest of war.

record high. Large numbers of people were being discharged from the D.C. area's mental hospitals with no place to go.

Luther Place Memorial Church was one of two inner city churches that opened its doors, allowing homeless people to sleep in the sanctuary. I volunteered at this church from 1977–78, when they were housing the homeless. After I graduated from college, still feeling compelled by their ministry and advocacy, I worked in their shelter for another year.

This was a church institution that was responding to basic human needs, having been pushed to do so by a smaller, more radical Christian community group. I saw an institution being changed. I was inspired.

During this period, CCNV continued its relentless pressure on the federal government until finally Ronald Reagan handed over one of D.C.'s buildings for shelter use. Today CCNV still operates this building, the largest homeless shelter in D.C. It is located on Mitch Snyder Avenue in honor of Mitch's relentless battle on behalf of those most in need in our city.

Through this experience, I learned that people of faith need to challenge institutions. I learned that the institutions we've created as a society (both nonprofit and for-profit), while necessary, often become entrenched and rigid. When focused on institutional survival they operate in direct opposition to the greatest needs of the people.

I learned that community organizing and public witnessing for social concerns are not only things that secular people do, but deeds that people of faith need to do as well. In fact, when people of faith get involved more actively, they renew the church.

I was inspired to hold onto my faith commitment, despite many of my friends leaving the church. I realized that faith communities like CCNV and Luther Place Memorial Church were lights to the rest of us, drawing us forward to stand up and be active peacemakers.

In 1982 my husband, Jim, and I joined the Sojourners Community.

We were both attracted to this ecumenical church community because it was actively pursuing peace and justice as a Christian calling. This group of people shared their income and homes in Southern Columbia Heights, a poor neighborhood in D.C. They were inspired by the early Christians in the book of Acts.

Many came to Sojourners who were disappointed with institutional churches (those affiliated with denominations) with budgets and paid pastors, meeting regularly on Sunday mornings in church buildings. We had similar feelings. I had learned to care about peacemaking growing up in the Mennonite Church, but wasn't drawn to the local Mennonite churches for worship and community, since they weren't as active in movements for social change.

We lived with the Sojourners Community from 1982 until 1990. It was a profound and enriching experience. Life in the community was vibrant for much of this time. However, things were also changing and people began leaving. By 1990, our family made the choice to leave as well. We had two children, ages five and two. We learned that many other Christian communities were breaking up also. One of the key reasons for the exodus was the toll it took on families, requiring many meetings to maintain the community. We also struggled with tensions about the direction and leadership of the community.

Despite the large exodus, the community continued meeting and worshipping together for many years. Although they no longer have an intentional community, the magazine and social justice advocacy of Sojourners continues.

After leaving the Sojourners Community, our family joined a new church in Maryland called Circle Community Church, made

up of many who had left the Sojourners Community. Our family moved to northeast D.C., near another family we had known at Sojourners. For ten years we were involved at Circle Community Church, with a collective focus on family and community, along with shared leadership in worship. We grew in our faith together and grappled with the injustices and violence in our world community. But eventually things changed and people began leaving.

During this time, around the year 2000, our family decided to join Hyattsville Mennonite Church. It was a big change for us. Even though we had not chosen to join a larger institutional church previously, we were now drawn to this church community due to its youth group, strong Sunday school program, and the emphasis on peace, justice, and personal faith. We were excited soon after we arrived that this church hired an outgoing pastor from Sojourners Community, Joe Roos.

Joe and his spouse, Cheri Herbolt, also an ordained minister, led the community through the 9/11 experience. Through their capable leadership, along with other pastors and lay leaders, we were strengthened in our understanding of Jesus' radical call. We believed his call to nonviolence meant our country should not retaliate for the attacks but instead offer peaceful solutions to the international conflicts which gave rise to the attacks.

As a continuing member at Hyattsville, I have been working with the Church of the Saviour community in Washington, D.C., since 2007. My role is Coordinator of the Discipleship Year Program, a voluntary service program placing persons in ministries.

Church of the Saviour, a collection of small faith communities founded in the 1940s, has created more than fifty nonprofit organizations which address poverty and injustice on many levels. Those involved with Church of the Saviour are invited to nurture their relationship with God, join a "mission group" of people with similar callings, and attend worship regularly.

In 1994, the Church of the Saviour became a "scattered community" of eight small faith communities. Today there are ten. Each of these churches is independently incorporated and seeks to embody its own unique vision, mission, and structure, while striving to maintain an "Integrity of Membership" in the spirit of the founding church.

The Church of the Saviour ecumenical headquarters building was sold recently and in December of 2010, Pastor Gordon Cosby retired from preaching on a regular basis. He was ninety-one at the time! This means there is no longer a legally owned and operated Church of the Saviour church building.

A Church of the Saviour "Ecumenical Council" meets regularly and is made up of representatives from the various churches founded in the tradition of the Church of the Saviour. They meet to discuss and discern the common concerns and interests of all the "scattered churches."

The disciplines of the members of these scattered churches include daily prayer, Scripture reading, and disciplines that help

them grow inwardly. Members tithe ten percent of their income and commit to a mission group that meets weekly, focused on the "outward part of the journey." Church of the Saviour interprets the call to discipleship as the integration of two journeys in community—an inward journey to grow in love of God, self, and others, and an outward journey to help mend creation.

Their programs provide health care, education, housing, employment, children's programs, drug and alcohol rehabilitation, AIDS home hospice, and much more for those in need in D.C. They operate the Potter's House, a coffee shop and alternative book store, where many of their small faith communities meet for worship. Other worshipping communities have sprung up and meet in other parts of the city.

The Festival Center, the building out of which I work, runs their Servant Leadership School (also called an alternative seminary), which teaches classes to deepen the Christian walk for both the inward and outward parts of our journey. Classes are taught on prayer, Scripture, calling, racism, economics, militarism, environmental concerns, and more. Festival Church, one of the scattered churches, meets here weekly. Additionally, ministries of the Church of the Saviour have office space in the Festival Center and spiritual support groups, recovery groups, and other churches use its meeting spaces.

Through race education, I'm convinced that all churches, including Hyattsville Mennonite Church, need to grapple more seriously with the call for Christians to break down race and class barriers. Currently a "race matters" group meets at Hyattsville and we grapple with how to address racism in our congregation. My hope is that this small group's emphasis and commitment will bring new life to the church community as well.

I believe that institutional churches and organizations can be revitalized. I also believe that sometimes old forms of church and community must die in order for new ones to emerge. If Christians are wise, we will recognize that this needs to happen. We can even help it happen. In other cases, institutions can be revitalized when people within them work together. We need to stay open and welcome fresh vision. We need to believe that God's Spirit will guide us into new territory. Otherwise, there is danger of becoming stagnant, cynical, and resigned to the way things are.

The Spirit is leading, and I trust that God will guide us into the future if we are open to God's vision. Let us not be afraid to challenge ourselves deeply and find ways to hold each other and ourselves accountable to the central messages in the gospel. May we all follow our callings and search for deep and true community that crosses lines of race and class. May we also engage with the institutions around us in loving and yet challenging ways.

CHAPTER NINE

CHRISTIAN PEACEMAKER TEAMS: The Journey of Liberation

by Tim Nafziger

Grounded in his personal experience and that of his mother, Tim Nafziger outlines the formation and ongoing work of Christians Peacemaker Teams. Working in an organization that started out as a movement, calling for active peacemaking in areas of conflict, he wrestles with the impact of organizational growth and change. Sharing stories of both personal and organizational transformation, he names the difficulty of partnerships across lines of privilege and disempowerment.

When I was nine, my mother, Lois Nafziger, became a Sunday school superintendent at River Corner Mennonite Church in Conestoga, Pennsylvania. It turned out to be a controversial decision: her aunt and family left the church. Lois was the first woman to fill that leadership role in the church. Though male leaders had been part of selecting her for this position, none of them defended her. I vividly remember the tearful conversations my mother had with her own mother at the time. For her whole life, my grandmother wore cape dresses and a covering. She struggled to understand my mother's calling beyond the constraints the church placed on her.

My mother grew up in a traditional Mennonite community, the eighth of eleven children, on a dairy farm a few miles outside Lancaster, Pennsylvania. She and her sisters grew up wearing cape dresses and coverings and learning that women's options in life were limited mainly to nurse, teacher, or mother. Like many her age, my mother stopped wearing a covering in the seventies but was still expected by the church to stay at home and raise my siblings and me. I was raised in the same church she grew up in, and I remember the older men and women still sitting on pews on opposite sides of the sanctuary.

In 1994, we left that community and moved to Goshen, Indiana, so my mother could get her master's in Peace Studies at Associated Mennonite Biblical Seminaries (Elkhart, Indiana). Three years later she joined Christian Peacemaker Teams, a decision that deeply shaped my life and vocation. In this chapter I'll share the story of my mother and myself, alongside the broader story of Christian Peacemaker Teams.

The founding of Christian Peacemaker Teams

In 1984, Ron Sider gave a speech to the Mennonite World Conference in Strasbourg, France. It came to symbolize the founding of Christian Peacemaker Teams. Sider laid out a grand vision of peacemakers by the hundreds of thousands descending onto conflict zones to bring justice to the downtrodden and peace to warring parties:

> Unless we . . . are ready to die by the thousands in dramatic vigorous new exploits for peace and justice, we should sadly confess that we never really meant what we said, and we dare never whisper another word about pacifism to our sisters and brothers in those desperate lands filled with injustice.[1]

For most Mennonites up to this point, alternatives to war had largely been framed in terms of voluntary service. Conscientious objectors during WWII and Vietnam spent their time quietly working as orderlies in hospitals or as part of the Civilian Conservation Corps in national parks. Sider's vision of stepping boldly onto the world stage as protectors of the poor and oppressed was exciting and deeply compelling. Anabaptist church leaders asked the Mennonite Central Committee's Peace Section to explore the idea further.[2]

Often overlooked are the stories of peace activists who had quietly been doing accompaniment work in conflict areas for decades. Hedy Sawadsky, CPT steering committee member from 1986 to 2010 is a good example of this pattern. *[See Chapter 5 for Hedy's story.]*

Similarly, Gene Stoltzfus and Dorothy Friesen worked alongside Filipinos, challenging the Marcos regime. Marilen Abesamis, a Filipina woman who worked with Gene and Dorothy, says, ". . . Gene's journey with us during those trying moments helped us immensely but also helped him in transforming his part of the world, and in his creative witnessing for global peace—reverberating as does the flutter of a butterfly, across the globe."[3]

One of those reverberations was the creation of Synapses, founded in 1981 by Gene and Dorothy, along with Joan Gerig and Orlando Redekopp after they returned from work with Mennonite Central Committee outside the United States. Synapses worked to support the struggle for peace and justice in the Philippines, Central America, and South Africa. Current CPT codirector Carol Rose and CPT training coordinator Kryss Chupp both worked with Synapses in the early eighties.

In 1983, Kryss and Gene were part of a delegation to Honduras and Nicaragua and saw firsthand the devastation of attacks by Contras funded by the U.S. government. The Contras were armed groups fighting to overthrow the Sandinista government in Nicaragua. The delegation also came face-to-face with the lies that propped up the war. "We talked about how you work with a government that is constantly lying," said Steve Wiebe-Johnson, who was on the trip. "How does the church respond?"[4]

But among historic peace churches, the gospel-rooted call to challenge the oppression of the U.S. government was limited to a small minority. Along with those already named above, Bob Hull, Peter and Mary Sprunger-Froese *[see Chapter 7 for Mary and Peter's story]*, Al Zook, and Peter Ediger were actively challenging U.S. militarism in many forms.[5] After Sider's speech, these activists, already committed to working for justice and challenging empire, realized there was an opportunity to draw in a wider group. The vision of peacemaking, they agreed, included tactics like nonviolent direct action and political advocacy.

In 1986, Gene helped to gather leaders from the historic peace churches, as well as activists, to talk about what this new movement might look like. As Gene later described this meeting at the Techny Towers in Chicago, "God granted a spirit of unity to the gathering of one hundred persons and a call went out for the formation of CPT."[6] Dorothy and Hedy, appointed as activist members-at-large of the first steering committee, worked hard in the planning meetings to keep CPT headed toward action and engagement with the world rather than "the production of peace literature."[7] In 1988, Gene was named director of the new organization.

Over the following years, CPT gathered energy and engaged with the broader peace churches (especially the Mennonites) through public actions at conventions and engagement with delegates. When I suggested in an email to Dorothy Friesen that CPT grew "on the margins of the established peace churches" she replied that "Gene never thought he was at the edge of the church, he saw himself at the core of Anabaptism."[8] As I reflect on this statement, I realize it was this audacity and strength that first drew me to CPT as a teenager.

From "vote Bush" to the School of the Americas

Growing up in Lancaster, I had absorbed the prevailing winds of Christian conservatism. I remember having arguments with my mom on the way home from church about whether women could be leaders in the church. Somehow, as a child and pre-adolescent I had a strong sense of the way things *ought* to be. In my mind, abortion was the only political issue that mattered. In 1992, I wrote "vote Bush" on small yellow Post-it notes and stuck them all over the house. When my parents confessed they had voted for Clinton, I was flabbergasted.

"Mennonite" was simply the ocean I swam in. It was all I knew at school, church, and family gatherings. I didn't have a strong sense of Mennonites as distinctive, since everyone around me was Mennonite. The community was very tradition-oriented.

Moving to Goshen changed that. I attended a public school for a year and began attending a church that was self-consciously Mennonite. I became friends with the grandnephews of John Howard Yoder and was in a small group with Mennonite seminary professors. I came to understand that Mennonites offered a distinctive perspective on the world.

As a teenager in 1997, I attended a national Mennonite gathering in Orlando and began developing a critical eye for the excesses of glitzy hotels and the contradictions of these gatherings. I also encountered Christian Peacemaker Teams for the first time, protesting Disney's treatment of Haitians in sweatshops where Disney apparel was made.

That fall I attended the annual vigil at the School of the Americas in Columbus, Georgia, where thousands of faith-based activists participated in a symbolic funeral procession and committed mass civil disobedience by crossing onto the military base where they were all arrested for trespassing. The experience was a catalyst for me, clarifying a strong sense of call to work for peace and social justice.

I also began to embrace a distinctive set of Anabaptist values as part of my faith. Like many Mennonites, moving out of a Mennonite enclave forced me to think about what my faith meant to me outside of a traditional farming context. Rather than orienting myself around family and tradition, I began to orient my life around values like justice and peace.

My mother joins CPT—I follow six years later

In September 1993, CPT held a training for the first members of its Christian Peacemaker Corps. Four years later in 1997, my mother went through the same month-long training program and joined CPT. During the training, she found kindred spirits:

> Each person told our faith journey. And my memory of that time is that we found that most of us were wounded peacemakers. We had challenges that we faced in our own lives. And they were as varied as the individuals who spoke. It was a time of tears and laughter. Of acknowledging who we were and who we had been. And that affirmation was critically important in turning us into CPTers.[9]

My mother's first stint as a CPTer was in Chiapas, Mexico, where she was part of the team's accompaniment of Las Abejas, an indigenous Catholic movement advocating for their rights. The group formed in 1992 to work together nonviolently for justice for their communities.[10] On December 22, 1997, Mexican para-military forces massacred forty-five members of Las Abejas during a prayer meeting while Mexican state police stood by.[11]

Las Abejas invited CPT to walk with them in their efforts to return to their villages and their struggle for autonomy for their communities. They faced regular harassment and threats from paramilitaries as well as Mexican military.

My mother, Lois, arrived on the team in 1999. She saw her role as a CPTer to be that of a witness. "In response to this horrible action by the paramilitary, the Las Abejas community joined together to address the injustices that were going on. They spoke to others in the community, they spoke to the churches, and they spoke to the government." she said. "Our goal was to amplify their voice in some way." Lois saw her role as learning from and about the struggle of Las Abejas and then taking their stories back to her home congregation, community, and political representatives.[12]

Lois also served on the CPT team in Pierre, South Dakota, in 1999, where CPT was accompanying members of the Lakota nation as they occupied an island. The occupation was in response to the Mitigation Act, a piece of legislation that moved two hundred thousand acres of land from federal to state hands. This legislation, pushed by Senator Tom Daschle and Governor William Janklow, was in contradiction to the Fort Laramie treaties of 1851 and 1868. CPT was invited by Lakotas Harley and Sue Eagle due to fears of retaliation from local white communities.[13]

Lois described the protective accompaniment element of the work: "The white community threatened the Lakota community to get them to leave. They didn't want them there making their claim to the land. I remember there were several all-night vigils while I was there, watching the entrance to the camp."[14]

Through my mother's experiences I got to know CPTers through the CPT Northern Indiana (CPTNI) regional group. I was drawn to their imaginative responses to injustice. When the KKK promised to picket outside an agency in Goshen that served the Latino community, CPTNI organized an ice cream social for the same time and place. When the local air force base christened a new B-2 bomber, we organized a B-2 bomber buyback program outside the gates and tried to interest the military police. I embraced a bold, creative Christian faith that was willing to take risks and challenge the powerful—to look them in the eye and respectfully but clearly denounce their greed, militarism, and fear mongering.

When I joined CPT as a reservist in 2003, I was committing to a community that had already deeply shaped my life. Through the mentoring of CPTers like my mother, Rich Meyer, Janet Shoemaker, and Cliff and Arlene Kindy, I discovered my own call to confronting injustice in my community, country, and the world. In the coming years, I would find CPT challenging me to look inward as well.

Growth, privilege, and accountability

Through the late 1990s and early 2000s, CPT grew rapidly from a small, relational network to a mid-size nonprofit with a budget of a million dollars. This growth meant shifts in decision-making styles. In the early days, the whole administrative staff (called the "support team") worked together in one room and the entire corps knew each other personally. When the corps tripled in size, handling situations on a case-by-case basis was no longer possible and CPT began to develop policies. Some of these policies, such as the one on sexual harassment, developed out of specific incidents. Others came out of a general sense of responsibility and the need for consistent organizational responses and just treatment of those inside (and outside) CPT. In some cases, creating a policy was important from an anti-racism perspective. In naming who was responsible for what decisions, CPT aimed to make decision making transparent. This also prevented power from pooling with those most embedded in CPT culture and those with white, North American privilege.

Though on the edges of their own communities due to their activist commitments, CPTers brought significant power and privilege with them to the communities they accompanied. In fact, early in CPT's history, participants saw their privilege as North Americans as part of what allowed them to do protective accompaniment of local activists. There was a dissonance for CPTers as they recognized that the privilege their work relied on was often based on the white U.S. imperialism they were working against. This problem became even more apparent in the early 2000s as Colombians joined the CPT team there.[15]

Milena Rincón was the first Colombian to serve on the Colombia team when she joined as an intern in January of 2003. In the summer of 2003, she went through the CPT training in Chicago to join as a full-time member of the team. "I understood the mission as a challenge for Christians, mostly from North America, to go beyond their concern for justice and peace and move into specific actions, that usually meant to go overseas to accompany communities," she said. "They came with good intentions and good hearts, but in many cases they did not understand the conflict, they didn't get truly involved with the communities, neither did they listen carefully to the community's wisdom about how to do peacemaking, and at the end they left the country with stories to share but with not much work in their own homes on how they need to act there."[16]

Milena and others began to look within CPT at the way the power and privilege of white North Americans permeated CPT's work. Two results of these efforts were the hiring of Sylvia Morrison in 2007 as the Undoing Racism Coordinator, and the anti-racism audit of the organization in 2008 and 2009. This audit culminated in a strategic planning process that resulted in seven strategic directions for CPT around Undoing Racism, including "honoring the voices of our partners throughout CPT communication vehicles" and "making all of CPT accountable to our partners in an open and transparent way." These goals are part of a shift away from seeing CPTers as central to the work and toward seeing local partners' peacemaking work as central.

CPT has worked hard to make it clear that CPTers are not superheroes, swooping in with all the peacemaking answers. "I believe that one of the most important changes has been CPT's commitment to understand better how privilege can get in the way of local efforts for peacemaking," Milena said. "In the Colombia project, the voice of the communities on how to build peacemaking has become stronger, and paying attention to that voice has led the team to offer better political and physical accompaniment."[17]

In the eight years I've been a part of the CPT corps, I've been consistently challenged to recognize the ways that I, as a straight white male, am complicit in militarism and oppression. But I am not left to stew in my guilt. Instead, I am invited into a grace-filled community of loving transformation where all are called to become allies in the work of resisting violence.

Milena addressed the 2009 Mennonite World Conference gathering in Paraguay as a way of marking twenty-five years since Sider's speech. In it she said:

> CPT has been a Christian organization that has traveled many paths, has made errors in judgment, has honored moments of grief, has worked through difficult situations, and has celebrated with joy events that arise from a deep commitment to Life. We have shared with visionary men and women whose accumulated life experiences challenge daily our faith and commitment to justice. Yes, we approached them believing that as Christians we would be the ones to help them, but that was not the case. The communities continually remind us that the commitment to justice and peace cannot be carried out by a small group of people with good intentions; rather it must happen in conjunction with the communities, the grassroots organizations and individuals who are convinced that nonviolence is a viable route to peace.[18]

As CPT's focus on Undoing Racism deepened, it began to illuminate the way white people within the organization held power and the patterns that maintained white privilege. There was also the question of how it shaped CPT's work externally. In both these areas, the work of Ann Bishop became important. Her book, *Becoming an Ally,* proposed a model for those with privilege to work alongside those who were oppressed.

CPT learnings, an offering to Mennonites

For over four hundred years, Mennonites have seen themselves as the persecuted minority; this is especially evident in *Martyrs Mirror* as well as in the stories of the Mennonites' exodus from the Ukraine less than one hundred years ago. But for most white U.S. and Canadian Mennonites, persecution is no longer their reality.

The Mennonites (and others) who founded CPT reexamined their self-image in light of their position in the heart of the U.S. and Canadian military and economic structures. First, drawing on liberation theology, they discovered a call to solidarity and resistance that acknowledged their privileged social position. From the beginning, this led to a focus on anti-racism, but over the past six years, there has been a clear call to deeper examination of the way white privilege has distorted our work and our community. I believe that many Mennonites in the United States would prefer to still see themselves as the victims in the engravings of *Martyrs Mirror* while ignoring (or even rationalizing) our complicity in ongoing acts of torture and dehumanization in Abu Ghraib and Guantanamo Bay.

Second, we Mennonites involved in CPT have not sought to label the enterprise "Mennonite." Instead, we have challenged ourselves to move beyond the white Mennonite cultural patterns that are familiar to us. In doing so, we have opened ourselves to recognizing the Spirit moving in other cultures and traditions without needing to label it "Mennonite" or even "Anabaptist."

We have come to recognize that it is not about us but about creating the space for the radical nonviolent witness of our partners to shine forth. When movements come along with the social and political disruption that the first Anabaptists knew, they will never be welcomed into existing structures of Mennonitism. If we are to join them, we must walk out our doors into new spaces of partnership: in the mountains of Iraqi Kurdistan, in the South Hebron hills, in the jungles of Colombia, or in the pine forests of Ontario.

CHAPTER TEN

MAPLE CITY HEALTH CARE CENTER: Dying to the Fear of Death

By James Nelson Gingerich

As the founding doctor of Maple City Health Care Center (MCHCC), James Nelson Gingerich developed his vision for alternative health care while living at the Bridge Street household in Goshen, Indiana, in the 1970s. In this chapter he challenges institutions specifically, but more generally any community, to be mission-driven rather than survival-driven. Through examples from MCHCC he illustrates what it means to be centered on relationships, to seek integration, and to be empowering as a community. Rooted in the Anabaptist tradition, his words are timely, as many organizations face tightened budgets and risk sacrificing their vision to stay alive.

Introduction

Years ago I participated in a community hospital board's strategic planning retreat. The conversation focused on identifying and exploiting the most profitable sectors of the local medical marketplace. Eventually someone asked whether in shaping strategic planning to maximize profits, we might be neglecting some aspects of the community's health, and especially the health of those who have the fewest resources. The hospital CEO's response was classic: "No margin, no mission." This kind of thinking has a "duh" quality about it. Isn't it obvious that if an organization folds for lack of income, its mission dies, too? But in response to the CEO's assertion, I blurted out, "No mission, no mission."

I don't think an organization can have it both ways. If we focus on margin, we jeopardize mission. As I have participated in a variety of community and church organizations over the years I have become more and more convinced that there are two kinds of organizations: the vision-driven ones and the funding-driven ones. Faced with decisions, the basic impulse, from which all else flows, is to ask one of two questions: Does this move make us more secure—more financially solvent or more profitable? Or does this move fit with our vision and our mission, our reason for being? Quite apart from the answers, our asking of either question sets fundamental direction.

The writer of Hebrews tells us that Jesus shared our flesh and blood so that he might destroy the one who has power of death "and free those who all their lives were held in slavery by their fear of death" (Hebrews 2:14-15 NIV). I wonder whether we apply this wisdom to our church bodies, our institutions, and our congregations. Do we believe in Jesus' power to free us institutionally from our bondage to the fear of death? Do we focus on institutional survival, or can we trust our organizations' future to God's provision and protection and instead focus on seeking God's reign and its justice?

Reinhold Niebuhr saw Jesus as articulating an ideal of indiscriminate love, of agape. He thought Jesus' love ethic wouldn't work for modern American Christians who, unlike Jesus, don't think the world is about to end and who believe they should take responsibility in society and for its institutions. According to Niebuhr, Jesus' "pure" ethic is still relevant as an ideal that shows the inadequacy of all our efforts and reminds us of our need for grace. It is also relevant (here I quote John Howard Yoder) as "a principle of discriminating criticism that helps us make relative judgments within the constraints of the possible, so we can do the best we can."[1] But it is not relevant in the sense that we can or should try simply to live by it; that would not be realistic or socially responsible.

Many North American Mennonite theologians and ethicists in the past half century have appreciated Niebuhr's critique of theological liberalism and his trenchant description of human nature and human sin. But some have argued against Niebuhr where he turns to sources for ethics that take us away from Jesus and sometimes toward justifying using violence, for example, as the "responsible" thing to do. Yet this thinking sometimes operates among church leaders in their exercise of their responsibilities.

I'm not opposed to being practical and fiscally responsible. I make budgets and watch bottom lines; I drive a hard bargain when negotiating agreements with laboratories and Medicaid contractors. But whenever I hear community or church leaders advocating a certain course of action because what is at stake is nothing less than the organization's survival—then I see red flags waving. I ask myself, what is being advocated here that would not otherwise seem justifiable? What are we being urged to do that is not consonant with our mission and identity?

Living into a vision

When I was barely thirty, I began my work with Maple City Health Care Center, believing that community engagement need not constrain our ethic to one of compromise for the sake of responsibility. Here I want to offer a look at the development of the health care center's vision—in fits and starts, through failure and anxiety, as well as in renewed energy and excitement and joy. It is a vision for a reconciling and healing community. This is not a result of programmatic activity but an expression, an integral part, of who we are becoming. In this vision I hope you will see relevance for the Mennonite church, for our congregations and our agencies, for grassroots initiatives, and for leaders and leaders-in-training in church and community.

From the beginning, I approached the work of Maple City Health Care Center as being about creating a space for people in a diverse but largely low-income neighborhood to come together in ways that would bring some measure of healing to us and to our community. This approach, coming out of my experiences of and convictions about the church, is rooted in my commitment to the Anabaptist tradition. The vision was about breaking down barriers and fostering a community of wholeness, integration, and healing.

At that time the primary diversity in the neighborhood was not ethnic and racial but socioeconomic. Our early vision statement talked about fostering healthy community by offering integrated primary care medicine in a neighborhood-based and community-oriented way. We also talked about offering health care that allowed middle-class folks and people in poverty to receive care side by side.

From the health center's beginning we had a sense that the integration we were trying to foster in our neighborhood had to be manifest in our staff structure. For our vision of community to become a reality, we needed to keep focused on it as our guide for everything. So we were not just concerned about making our health care affordable. We also wanted to make sure all our staff members were receiving livable wages and that wage and wealth disparities among our staff were minimized. Benefits were also generous and shared, so all could live with a sense of security and of having enough.

Sometimes matters that were clear to me were much less clear to members of our board. It took time and careful listening to find common ground. When in board meetings I would talk about preventive care and fostering community, low-income board members would say that the thing they wanted most in a health care center was to have a doctor willing to see their child when she was sick, and to be able to afford to pay the bill. We had conversations over a matter of months about whether we wanted to be a health care provider of last resort, only taking care of poor people, or whether we, having located our center in the town's lowest-income neighborhood, wanted to serve that neighborhood as a whole, regardless of residents' income: Did we want to be a resource the community could take ownership in, or would we be a place where only the desperate sought help?

I suppose that way of framing the alternatives tells you what we decided. Early on, we developed the sense that we exist to serve a vision for community. We wanted that vision to guide everything we did, not just in developing programs, but in determining the funding we would seek, how we would structure and recruit staff, and how the staff and board would function. Vision was central, and in our decision-making discussions, an appeal to vision was a trump card anyone could play. On the other hand, any argument in which we needed to set aside vision for the sake of survival was immediately suspect. We would not compromise vision for matters of practicality.

Engaging asset-based community development

In the mid-1990s, I attended a Healthy Communities Summit in San Francisco. It was my first sustained exposure to asset-based community development. Those who adopt this approach focus not on a community's problems but on its assets. They foster and build on the gifts and strengths already present in a community. As John McKnight has written:

> Care is. . . the manifestation of a community. The community is the site for the relationship of citizens. And it is at this site that the primary work of the caring society must occur. If that site is invaded, co-opted, overwhelmed, and dominated by service-producing institutions, then the work of community will fail.[2]

This approach raised the question: How can we foster becoming a site for relationship among neighbors rather than being a service-producing institution?

Four learnings came from this exposure: First, a community organizer from South Central Los Angeles told us: "If you only remember one thing, remember this: Whatever you focus on is going to multiply. If you focus on your community's needs and problems, they will multiply. If you focus on the little signs of hope, they will multiply." Second, this summit stressed the conclusions of recent studies indicating that social isolation all by itself is a huge risk factor for poor health and early death. Just helping people connect with each other could be a strategy for fostering both personal and community health. A third learning we took from this event was an asset-based approach to hiring staff. Instead of hiring people from a pool of applicants, we began recruiting people who share our commitments. Our commitment to our staff, then, was to foster their potential for our mutual benefit. A fourth learning was to pay attention to imagination as one of our assets. We began to see the importance of making space for imagination and innovation, of fostering a community of imagination and even risk-taking.

These learnings gave us a new framework to talk about many things we'd already been doing. In focusing on the neighborhood instead of just poor people, we chose be an asset for the community, not merely a place for the desperate to bring their problems. We had already been recruiting staff for their vision and commitments, not just for their marketable skills. We had already been thinking imaginatively both as staff and board.

Nontraditional "health" care

Our new way of thinking helped us recognize nontraditional encounters as a part of health care, but we struggled to fully integrate such
encounters into our organizational identity.

During this time, one of our patients, an isolated teenager, began
breaking into the health care center now and then at night. There
seemed to be no malice in it: he stole a few dollars, played with
some of the equipment, left us notes. Eventually the police caught
him there and arrested him. Dan, one of our board members who
often volunteered at the center, worked with the prosecutor, and
eventually the court sentenced Tony (not his real name) to two
hours a week of community service at the health care center. He
came sullenly and half-heartedly did the tasks we assigned.

One week he showed up to work on a Wednesday afternoon,
when a cooking group was meeting there. Someone in the group
noticed Tony and invited him to join them for their meal. He took
off but reappeared a few minutes later with some banana bread
from home. From then on, he did his community service on Wednesday afternoon, and he stayed for the shared meal. His disposition
changed, as did his work habits.

Before long, Tony had completed his court-mandated community service, but he kept coming on Wednesdays, now as a volunteer
and to eat with the group. We laughed when he told us that he'd
started to patrol the area at night with his dog, so there wouldn't
be any trouble with people breaking in. One week he announced
that he'd made the honor roll at school for the first time, and we
celebrated with a party. Tony finished high school on schedule and
went on to study at a community college. Now he works for the
local newspaper.

Although our staff had been providing standard medical care
for Tony for years, his break-ins eventually convinced us that we
were not addressing what really ailed him. And our contributions to his eventual healing were not the result of our program as
much as the fruit of impulses among people—mostly volunteers
and patients—who came together at the center to reach out and
include one another. In the end, the staff mostly provided space
and looked on as patients and volunteers took Tony in and gave
him a sense of belonging and purpose. Tony's steps to a healthier

life seemed to happen despite our programmatic (medical) activity, not because of it. Through his example we recognized the non-traditional relationship building as being at the heart of what we wanted to be about.

Guiding questions

Then one year I attended a Mennonite Health Assembly meeting that featured Doug Eby, a Mennonite physician who led a restructuring of Native American health services in Alaska. Over about a dozen years, he helped transform that system from a typical bureaucratic clinic structure into a native-owned and operated system of care. One result was a huge improvement in patient access. But Eby says, "It's not about access. It is only through solid relationships that you can begin to get at insidious underlying health issues such as depression, domestic violence, and obesity."

Through our exposure to Doug Eby's story we found a straightforward approach to discernment about what we are trying to do, by asking three questions of everything we do: Does it foster long-term relationships? Does it increase integration? Does it empower people? These themes were already present in our approach, but this new shorthand gave us a tool to use consistently and broadly.

We began explicitly asking these questions of all programmatic initiatives, of all funding initiatives, of all policy proposals. We even restructured our employee evaluations around these questions: (1) What about your job fosters long-term relationships with patients, with other staff, with members of the community? And what about your job gets in the way of such relationships? (2) What about your job fosters integration of care for patients? your integration into the staff? your integration into the community? your personal integration (job and rest of life)? And what about your job gets in the way of such integration? (3) What about your job is empowering for you? empowering for others? What about your job is disempowering?

Creating a shared community

The other transformative thing that Doug Eby shared was his call to escape the "tyranny of the traditional physician-patient encounter." This one-on-one, private, behind-closed-doors encounter, characterized by huge power differentials, is fundamentally opposed to community-building. It does not tend to foster authentic long-term relationships. It does not tend to empower patients. And it is therefore unlikely to foster integration between medical encounter and needed lifestyle changes.

So we began to explore models for providing health care in groups. We had had groups: prenatal classes, mom-to-mom groups, support groups for survivors of sexual abuse, and the cooking group. And our board meetings and staff meetings were group activities. But all these were on the margins of the health care we offer. We had never tried to address health care itself in a group model.

We started our group efforts in two areas. First we explored an approach to prenatal care called Centering Pregnancy: pregnant women whose babies are due at about the same time meet together eight times. The role of staff is not to teach or bring expert opinion to bear on every question but to facilitate participation of all the members of the group.

We've learned to ask open-ended questions. I used to ask, "Are you planning to breastfeed?" Now I might ask, "What have you been thinking about feeding your baby?" Now the group can enter into a lively discussion of their experiences and their cultural assumptions. These discussions don't always promote the official line, but almost always we can talk with openness and validation of the perspectives of those around the circle.

Initially we conducted some groups in English and some in Spanish. But soon we found we did not have enough pregnant English-speaking patients to offer English-only groups. So we decided to try to have bilingual groups, with everything being interpreted both ways. We were afraid that all the bilingual interpreting might be cumbersome and ungainly, but we also saw the potential for cross-cultural bridge-building, and the development of new relationships. I started the first bilingual group by observing that the children whose births we are preparing for will likely play with each other, go to school with each other, and may eventually start new families together—so we want to prepare a shared community to receive them.

We were surprised to discover that the discipline of interpreting everything into English and Spanish, far from being intrusive and awkward, helped us listen better. People can only speak about one breath before they need to wait for translation. And only one person can speak at a time. So people speak with greater care and listen more carefully. And the subjects of pregnancy, childbirth, breastfeeding, childcare, and parenting, which are deeply lodged in a cultural context, provide opportunity for profound cross-cultural learning.

Reforming the agenda

One day I was writing a grant application. One question was, "How does your board reflect the diversity of your patient population?" I gulped. "It doesn't" didn't seem like a promising answer. It wasn't that we didn't want lower-income and non-Anglo members on our board. When the healthcare center was forming a decade and a half earlier, we had gathered community leaders of various classes and subcultures to form a board. As we generated ideas, made plans, raised funds, and rehabbed a building, there were plenty of ways for all kinds of people to get involved and contribute.

As the years went by, though, the work of the board became a matter of gathering for monthly meetings to oversee operations, approve budgets, and establish policies. Looking back, I began to realize that what we had tried was a classic approach to board function that relied on middle-class white assumptions about how you do business. You develop an agenda and you proceed through it in an orderly fashion, discussing each item and making decisions where necessary. The non-middle-class members had been committed enough to the health care center that they hung in there for a while with a board organization and process that was foreign to them, but eventually they had drifted away.

What else could we do? Did we want to invite people back into a structure they find alienating and disempowering, or could we rethink how we do our work at the board level? We began to ask ourselves, where in our organization is cross-cultural and socio-economically diverse group process happening most effectively? The clear answer was, in Centering Pregnancy groups. Then we asked, how can we build on that success and carry it over into our board organization and process?

At that point, we had a board composed of six middle-class Anglos—wonderful people, deeply committed to the organization— and two staff members. Organizationally we were not in crisis and could with openness and some excitement begin to reimagine the board's shape. We decided to experiment with borrowing the Centering Pregnancy circle model of group interaction and facilitative leadership, especially as we had adapted the model to cross-cultural groups.

We invited four people to join a reconstituted board: an Anglo single mother of seven, a factory worker who had been involved in student organizing as a youth in Mexico City, an employed Latina mother of two who had participated in a Centering Pregnancy group, and another young Latina mother. All four were patients, and we selected them after inviting our whole staff to consider the question: Which of our patients is deeply involved in the life of our neighborhood and brings passion and energy to their interactions at the health care center?

We gave up our agenda-driven meetings and instead now start each meeting with an extended conversation around the circle exploring how we relate to our community. A meeting might begin with: Tell us about what it is like to be a longtime resident—or a new immigrant—in this community. Where do you feel connected? Isolated? Alienated? All our conversations take place at table, around good food, and they are blessed by the slow process of English-Spanish and Spanish-English interpretation.

When we get around to addressing what would have been traditional agenda items, we treat them as housekeeping matters. If we have been attending to our relationships and our mission, our decisions are usually self-evident and take minimal time. And near the end of each meeting we go around the circle and ask, so what would you like to have in the record of this meeting? In a few minutes we decide what to record about what we've discussed and decided on.

We try to stay within our two-hour time limit for meetings, but invariably people stick around to help with dishes, or just to chat. One board member told us not long ago, "This is the most civilized part of my life. At work I'm in the jungle. Here we listen." Several members have remarked that nowhere else do they interact at such depth with people whose experiences and perspectives are so different from their own.

Conclusion

All of us are familiar with the progression from idealistic initiative or movement, to the bureaucratic shape institutions eventually take. We even accept as necessary a certain organizational "maturation," like the one Max Weber has described, from the charismatic to the bureaucratic. I wonder whether that progression doesn't coincide with, or develop out of, a shift from initial clarity of purpose to a focus on institutional survival. That shift I believe is deadly to our imagination and consigns us to a kind of living death.

If we want to avoid that kind of dying—as churches, as communities, as institutions—I think we need to name our fear of death and focus on survival as temptations from which we daily pray to be delivered. When we start talking about being realistic, practical, and responsible, we need to consider whether we are moving away from dependence on God and are trying instead to secure our own future. We need to recognize and name as seductive that siren song of survival, and listen to those who question where it calls us to go.

Indeed, within the first generation of Anabaptists, we see a people who unflinchingly faced death. In their example we encounter a mission—faithfulness to Christ—far outweighing bodily survival. Although for North American Anabaptist Mennonites the stakes are not often that high, their example calls us to examine assumptions about the survival of our institutions in this time of shifting economic and religious realities.

I believe that any organization that wants to take its inspiration from and orient its future toward a vision of a new reality needs to encourage and bless those who can help us stay focused on that vision. We need to heed those who invite us to be imaginative about our strengths and resources and possibilities, however challenging their words may be. And, if my experience is any gauge, we will watch those possibilities multiply, and we will rejoice in the abundance God provides.

Part Three

THIRD WAVE
(1990s *to* Present)

CHAPTER ELEVEN

MENNONITE VOLUNTARY SERVICE: A Jubilee Vision in Elkhart, Indiana

By Sarah Thompson

Beginning in 2007, the multiracial neighborhood of south central Elkhart, Indiana, has been home to the Jubilee House, a Mennonite Voluntary Service (MVS) Unit. Sarah Thompson, who grew up in Elkhart and lived at the Jubilee House, reflects on MVS through this lens. Since its inception in the 1950s, MVS has offered an opportunity for Christian intentional community living and has challenged the church to discipleship in many ways.

A Jubilee vision

On a gloriously damp Wednesday night, the community meal is in full swing. Jesi smiles and leans back in her chair. A young boy reaches across her plate for another handful of tortilla chips. She says, "I have never in my whole life come to a place and felt so welcome and accepted. . . and met so many people who smile so much. This place is crazy!"

Jesi lives in the neighborhood surrounding the Jubilee Mennonite Voluntary Service unit. Jubilee House is the current manifestation of MVS in Elkhart, Indiana. It is a large home across the south alley from Prairie Street Mennonite Church. The name *Jubilee* reflects the celebratory aspect of economic balance where debts are forgiven, captives are set free, and the favor of the Lord abounds. Jesus proclaimed these words in his first sermon (Luke 4:18-19), and invites his disciples throughout the ages to follow in his way, doing this work. Living into this reality is part of why the residents of Jubilee House smile so much and seek to welcome each person who passes through their door.

Without the practice of jubilee in U.S. American society, the gap between rich and poor widens every day. This gap is felt intimately in Elkhart. Even before the nationwide financial meltdown of 2008, south central Elkhart already experienced sustained economic poverty. Many people lack access to meaningful wage-labor, many are in financial debt, and others lack official U.S. documentation. These conditions often produce fragmentation, despair, and resignation in the neighborhood.

At various points in the history of the neighborhood, these conditions also catalyzed neighborhood action. Residents came together numerous times over the last twenty-five years seeking to receive a fair share of resources from city hall, to save Roosevelt Elementary School from demolition, and to counter environmental racism. Community meal, a weekly event hosted by the residents of Jubilee House, is another such community response. It is an embodiment of the justice and hope of the *jubilee* vision.

The division between MVSers as "givers" and neighbors as "receivers" begins to dissolve as we sit beside one another around the potluck. We believe that everyone has something to offer at community meal, whether it's the food they bring or their willingness to wash the dishes. Often, informal meetings are held after community meal, building on the connections made there, strengthening the neighborhood associations.

Examining Mennonite Voluntary Service

In this chapter, I will share some of the story of south central Elkhart and the Jubilee House and examine how the national MVS program has both grassroots and Mennonite institutional components. Since Elkhart Jubilee House is the MVS unit that I know best, I will examine this question from that context. Eighteen volunteers (and associate MVSers) lived in the house in its current status as part of the national MVS program, beginning in 2007. Since then, there have been as few as two—and as many as ten—people participating in MVS in Elkhart at any given time.

Though this chapter reflects on the early years of the Jubilee House, the work continues, not frozen in time by the writing. In preparation for writing this chapter, I conversed with each person who volunteered between 2007 and 2011, some neighbors, members of the MVS support committee and former MVS directors. Their stories moved me beyond words. Reflecting together about our experiences (of marathon-length house meetings, community celebrations, and gardening) deepened my perspective and humbled me.

Much like the Mennonite churches in the United States, MVS is part of a movement and part of an institution. Participants experience the more institutional or the more grassroots aspects in various ways. MVS both pushes the church and is nurtured by the church. Interested people over the age of twenty can become a volunteer (MVSer) and are invited to live into a different reality and life rhythm than what is offered in this increasingly fragmented, technological world. At its best MVS provides a house to live in, a community to be a part of, a vocation to test, space for conversation, and permission to push and question. There are MVS units across the country, each with distinctive characteristics.

South central Elkhart is a gem for the Midwest in terms of housing integration. Though with a high rate of resident turnover, there is an even mix of white, Latino, and black folks, with also a few Arab and Asian families. Its non-economic assets are immense. It's the next-door neighborhood to where I grew up, and as far back as I can remember, people from all ethnicities have often been willing to work together to achieve community goals. This willingness, along with immeasurable assets of roses shared from backyard plots, skilled childcare providers, well-attended basketball games, and bilingual children made it a dynamic place to grow up, as well as a place that I wanted to return to after university. From late 2007 to early 2009, I lived in Jubilee house and attended my home congregation, Prairie Street Mennonite Church.

As an MVSer I served at the Elkhart County Women's Shelter and taught Spanish classes. In addition to those placements, MVSers in Elkhart may work at organizations such as Church Community Services, Wheelchair Help, Elkhart Local Food Alliance, and Center for Community Justice. The money that each organization can contribute for the work of the volunteer goes into a common purse at Jubilee House, out of which residents buy food, pay rent, and provide small monthly stipends to each volunteer.

Because of the impact of systemic injustice on the neighborhood, at least one MVSer works as a community organizer. They use their days to build relationships with folks all over the neighborhood and learn about grassroots community efforts for justice. Since most church members do not live in the immediate neighborhood, the organizer also creates awareness and discussion in the local church context about the pertinent issues faced by neighbors. The community organizer position in Elkhart is unique among MVS units nationwide. A position like this succeeds in Elkhart because of the small size of the city, the history of Mennonite church organizers, and several volunteers' passion for the importance of movement building, anti-oppression work, and consciousness-raising.

Neighbors and sponsoring churches (Prairie Street Mennonite and Fellowship of Hope Mennonite Church) provide gracious hospitality, financial support, and moral encouragement to the changing residents of the unit. As a result of both this hospitality and patient organizing, MVSers now not only see their neighbors at the social service agencies where MVSers work, but in such contexts as the community entertainment event of "Cornbread and Jazz" and at the Summer Academy. Summer Academy is one effort that many sectors of the population worked together to plan and implement in response to their concerns about a lack of constructive, affordable, and educational activities for young people in the summer.

A history of hospitality

Although the unit began in 2007, MVS is not a new idea around Elkhart. The program's administration worked in the city from 1954–1974. There was also an MVS-like intentional community unit in Elkhart for a few years in the 1980s. The primary goal of establishing MVS units in the 1950s was to give young people in the Mennonite Church an opportunity to serve the world, wrestle together in community with big theological and social questions, and craft Mennonite faith responses to those questions.

MVS began as one of the tangible ways to maintain the commitment to Christian pacifism even in the context of national call to arms. When Mennonite men were drafted during the United States' involvement in World War II, some became conscientious objectors and completed service work in various locations throughout the United States. Women were not drafted at that time, but some women who loved and knew those men took the initiative to start volunteering in other life-affirming ways in the same communities where Mennonite men served. This caught on across the country and was sustained even after the end of World War II. The peak of participation of young people in MVS was during the United States' involvement in the war in Vietnam.

MVS in its current form is the confluence of several expressions of service and intentional community programs started by various Mennonite denominations in the United States MVS is one of the programmatic ways in which "the (bike tire) rubber meets the road" for its participants (about three thousand since 1943) as they have gained experience living out Christian faith with an emphasis on Mennonite practice. Along with spontaneity, creativity, and presence, simplicity in lifestyle is a hallmark value of the MVS program.

Between movements and institutions

I participated in MVS for just over one year. It was one of the most intense and formative years of my young adult life. Listening to other Elkhart MVSers share about their experiences, these sentiments arise for them, too. Though at times we felt plunged underwater by the weight of the issues we faced, the program provided for such things as fun time together and a mid-year retreat.

The daily rhythm of life in the Jubilee MVS unit creates layers and layers of accumulated experiences for its residents and visitors. Some experiences are magnificent, such as the formation of new friendships and when one can feel the power of the Spirit creating fearless community despite the odds. Some experiences are excruciating, such as sorting through multiple miscommunications that can happen, and result in hurt feelings, disillusionment, or deep confusion if not honestly and painstakingly addressed.

As MVSers experience transformation through their year of voluntary service, they challenge the entities around them to embrace the challenge of transformation as well. Because of the new perspective they bring, MVSers help local congregations by noticing and naming the patterns of interaction they see, both inside and outside the church. For example, a volunteer at Jubilee who is especially passionate about church helps Prairie Street Mennonite Church to think more intentionally about how church members interact with neighborhood children who attend church without their parents.

This agitation toward transformation is visible throughout the years of the MVS program. MVS volunteers have always pushed the envelope, such as in the areas of church planting and involvement in social movements. MVSers have changed the Mennonite church locally and nationally, and continue to influence it.

MVSers across the country are in a unique position, in a space between movements and institutions. From where they are they can bring to light "hot topics" and unaddressed issues of injustice. "MVSers," said one former director, "seek to be relevant and responsive." Elkhart is no exception to this statement, and there were so many days that I breathed a deep sigh of gratitude as I pulled up to the house on my bike. It was an immense encouragement to know that I lived in a household of people who cared so much about their relationships with God, each other, and the earth. And they were also fabulous cooks, activists, dumpster divers, theologians, artists, and musicians.

Local power and hospitality

Elkhart does not have the draws of urbanity as do the New York, Chicago, or San Francisco units. There is also no anonymity in this small city of 62,000. This feeling of always needing to be ready to extend or receive hospitality made it difficult for some to relax or feel okay about taking time to be by themselves. It was a hard balance to strike, and people did this in different ways.

For me, the lack of anonymity was a blessing in a time of need. For example, once in the local grocery store on my week to shop for the household, I accidentally purchased more food and fruit than I could carry home on my bicycle. I had left my cell phone at home, so I couldn't call anyone to come pick me up in the van. But I wasn't worried. I knew that if I simply waited outside the store, it wouldn't be too long before someone who had visited us at community meal or for a neighborhood meeting would come by and ask if I needed help.

Sure enough, within seven minutes I had an offer. It was from Paul, an actor and real estate agent who teaches the youth drama classes during Summer Academy. We had played tennis a few times, and he also attended the community Spanish classes I taught as part of my volunteer activities. The point of these classes was to increase community cohesion through building bridges by learning another neighbor's language. Prairie Street Mennonite Church already offered English classes for the growing population of Spanish-speaking adults; the Spanish classes were companion classes to that program. As we traveled back toward Jubilee House, Paul enthusiastically recited to me a few of the vocabulary words he had retained from the classes, and about a simple conversation that he had with the Latino family that lived across the street.

Recruiting people from the area (like me) who have a variety of existing relationships, counteracts the traditional North American service tendencies in which volunteers come for a short time and then leave the area after the required time of service. It also increases the accessibility of the unit to all people, not only college-educated young adults who can afford to live for a year or two outside their community.

Local recruitment is also an effort to reduce the strain on local agencies that traditionally must do a lot of sensitizing of volunteers who are new to the area and its social issues. It can take agencies a while to train volunteers well, only to have volunteers depart in a year because their term ended! Our approach has enabled deeper connections on multiple levels and more successful community organizing.

Inviting people new to the area as well as those familiar with it also introduced a power dynamic. Those who were local had more power than those who were not from the area. In some ways it was okay that those volunteers with more local connections had more power, because they often had a better sense of what was happening on multiple layers of the community. However, this dynamic was at times difficult to talk about within the household, depending on people's personalities, assumptions, and confidence. As one recent volunteer said,

> It was difficult at first to find my footing amongst these already established relationships and community ties and also to adjust to collective ways of thinking and taking care of Jubilee House and ourselves. However, this struggle has been worth it, because it has been good to get to

> know this different mix of people. . . and to learn to live
> together and challenge one another in our thinking.

In any new setting, one must learn to navigate the dynamics of established relationships and networks of care. MVS in Elkhart gives some a strenuous introduction to this. Others who hold relational power already have a different challenge. They have the opportunity to show hospitality and be informed and transformed by the different perspectives of new people.

Though Elkhart can boast having Jim Bixler, an MVS volunteer of fourteen years who works at the MC USA offices, the MVS program targets young adults who are experiencing a lot of change in their lives. As one of my housemates in 2008 said, "If you think you have it all together, MVS will show you that you do not."

Some people greatly admire the Jubilee House residents. Some think our efforts are a waste of time as far as gaining money is concerned. (An associate MVSer option now allows someone to be part of the household but not a part of the common purse, allowing for employment or schooling to happen at the same time as an MVS term). As MVS recruitment continues, the power of college debt to restrict many people is evident. Many do not feel like they can come to MVS after college if they have significant debt.

Though many volunteers do carry college debt, nearly all carry a college degree. How MVSers understand their power as college-educated predominantly white people in the midst of a mostly brown, non-college educated, working class community is a constant topic of conversation. Intentionally naming the types of interpersonal power and systematic privilege involved in any given situation is a regular practice. At times, discernment in conversation with neighbors and housemates as to how to act in a given situation also happens. I have seen God's powerful transforming love open up surprising possibilities for individual and community health when volunteers were willing to take the risk to make themselves vulnerable to these types of conversations.

Limitations in hospitality

Can only youth from economically comfortable families give a year for service, living in voluntary poverty? MVS is not a realistic choice for young people with financial obligations. The sometimes unnamed cultural and theological assumptions are also present in MVSers; these create barriers between them and others as they interact with differently-socialized people in their units and neighborhood. Jubilee House residents in Elkhart inadvertently fall into patterns that repeat exclusive practices. This is not always due to a lack of goodwill or dedication to reducing the participation barriers.

Questions arise about who MVS caters to and how to make it a program that is more welcoming, particularly to youth of color, poor people, and more religiously conservative people. These are ongoing questions for the program administration to address. They are issues that each local unit can also address. Issues of theology, access, and economic injustice do not disappear quickly and require careful and courageous conversation from all parties. Developing an analysis of the way systemic oppression functions in the United States (i.e., racism, sexism, classism, heterosexism, and U.S. exceptionalism) was very nurturing for some in Jubilee House.

Shaped by Jubilee

On another Wednesday night, an MVSer hands Jesi some forks to put on the table. She laughs, "I counted the forks in your drawer, and there weren't this many before. Somehow you always have enough forks for everyone who comes to the meal. . . it's the miracle of the forks!" God's abundance is palatable at Jubilee House.

The stories and analysis I have shared arise out of the emotionally, physically, and spiritually intense experience of living in intentional community and volunteering in a dynamic locality. They are hard for me to hold together at times. The impact of a year or two of MVS in Elkhart is best seen in the character, patterns, and language of current and former volunteers. May these reflections provide a glimpse into the beauty and difficulty of participation in a program that builds on and challenges Anabaptist faith and the practice of service.

CHAPTER TWELVE

URBAN VILLAGE: Becoming a Priesthood of All Believers

By Bert Newton with Joe Bautista

Following a Sunday school series on sustainable living grounded in Christian faith at Pasadena Mennonite Church in the late 1990s, a group of people asked what it would look like to "live it out." The answer led to the formation of the Urban Village community in Pasadena, California. From the beginning Urban Village has focused primarily on nurturing healthy relationships within the community, rather than focusing on activism outside the community. In this chapter, community members past and present reflect on their life together.

Introduction

One of our community members, Bob Nolty, often reminds us that "in theory, theory and practice are the same. In practice, theory and practice are always different."

In theory, Anabaptist churches practice the "priesthood of all believers," a biblical ideal that endows all members of the community equally with the power, authority, and responsibility to care for each other, speak for God, and minister to the world. In practice, some people turn out to be "more equal than others" (to borrow a phrase from George Orwell's *Animal Farm*). In practice, some people carry more power and influence, and some people's needs get overlooked.

When we formed the Urban Village community here in Pasadena, California, twelve years ago, we set out to be a community of shared life and witness, and we were fiercely egalitarian in theory, seeking to equally care for each other and empower each other to minister in the world. As we look back over the last twelve years, we ask ourselves, "How well did we accomplish this task?"

Our theory was that by living in closer proximity, we could have a greater shared life so that we could more effectively support each other, provide healing for each other, learn from each other, be discipled by each other, and be empowered to minister to the wider society.

Another one of our members, Joe Bautista, and I interviewed each member of our community, asking each person to give their perspective on how effectively we have practiced this "priesthood of all believers."

Before we get to the responses gleaned from these interviews, however, let me briefly describe our community so that you have some context for the comments that follow. The Urban Village was birthed out of Pasadena Mennonite Church but has become an ecumenical community with the largest contingent of non-Mennonites being Catholic. We continue to be active in our respective conventional churches, so our community is "parachurch."

Although we attempted to buy property together where we could all live, financial realities led us to settle for finding apartments and houses along one block of northwest Pasadena that we could move into as they became available. The garage of one of those houses, the only one owned by some community members, has been converted into our central meeting place.

Our life together has included prayer and worship, common study and learning, retreats, community engagement, recreation, and some types of economic sharing such as a car co-op and mutual aid.

Our outreaches have included block parties, tutoring, a theater troupe, community organizing around affordable housing, participation in the New Sanctuary Movement, volunteering in local homeless shelters, neighborhood food distribution, and initiating a local ecumenical peace march that has become an annual tradition.

In the interviews we conducted with current and past members of the community, we found that the question we were asking was answered in two ways: How have we been priests to each other, and how have we been priests to the rest of the world? So the reactions to the questions have been divided into two sections, the inward priesthood and the outward priesthood.

We found that our community members were far happier with what we've accomplished in our inward life than in how we've fared in ministering to the outside world.

Inward

All of those interviewed reported feeling that the community has had a fairly healthy inward dynamic, with most making almost glowing statements about it.

Dave, a founding member of the community, described the Urban Village as "an extension of my own family. . . and it serves the same function. . . always there in case something goes right; in case something goes wrong, they're there. . . it's a caring family."

Melissa, a graduate student who lived in the neighborhood and participated in the community for about three years before graduating and moving out of state, concurred that Urban Village acted as an extended family for her. She stated that for those three years, she spent Christmases with the community rather than going home to her biological family. Melissa reported that she had come out of a fairly negative intentional community experience but found healing and growth in Urban Village.

Melissa related that she was sad when her mother gave her a vacuum cleaner because, before then, she had been borrowing one from another household in the community, and borrowing the vacuum cleaner was always a good pretext for visiting with other community members.

Craig, a current community member for many years, described the community as "bright, warm, hopeful, peaceful, full of laughter, love and light. . . a refuge from the brutality of my work environment."

Christy and Aaron, a couple who lived with the community for several years before moving out of state, sent their response by email:

> Our experience in Urban Village was a very unique one, and is something that we still value and treasure to this day. It is something that we have found is not only sorely

missed in our lives, but is very special and is something that cannot be replicated.

We got married on the front lawn of the Vrede House [one of the UV houses] on Labor Day 2004. We laughed a lot and spent many nights talking, playing games, making funny videos, and of course having great fellowship. We also went through hardships together. We cried and mourned, we danced around a tree, we prayed and comforted, consoled each other and counseled each other.

Aaron added,

Most importantly UV was a family to me when mine was falling apart. If there was chaos in my life, which at that time was pretty much every day, the UV family was always there.

The most important thing about the intentional community was the closeness and the consistency of proximity. We were almost always together in one way, shape, or form. I look back now and realize that at times I took for granted just how much the community meant to me, and how difficult has been to form relationships outside of it. . . I would just say that UV was a special bond and place for me that transcended friendship and sometimes even family. It was the first place where I truly found God and godly living among real people. I will always treasure that special place.

Donna, someone who lives nearby and has been hanging out with the community fairly regularly for the last several years, described her experience this way.

I don't come from a Mennonite background. I grew up in an interdenominational evangelical framework of the go-out-and-be-the-salt-of-the-earth bent, and also moved around a lot, so the notion of a fixed and socially inward-facing community has been a somewhat foreign concept to me. As an adult I became confirmed as an Episcopalian and in that context have taken part in study groups that were intensive and transformative but did not yield ongoing contact.

I began to meet with Urban Village during a long and solitary convalescence and with specific physical limitations.

Perhaps the most significant thing for me about being with the group has to do with hospitality: the regularity of sharing a meal with the same people on a weekly basis, being greeted cheerfully when I arrive, and being given the prerogative to choose the seating that is most comfortable for me. "Just as I am. . ." I know it has been somewhat unusual for them to have someone around for several years who has not signed the group's covenant to become a formal member, in spite of which the stability, acceptance, and accommodation afforded to me have been a great encouragement. I don't experience the same closeness in the group that I have with other friends, but I feel strengthened by the commitment, discipleship, and social justice activities of the group's members, and challenged to remain faithful in my own Christian journey.

Anne, one of the newer members of the community, described her experience of coming into the community as being a little bumpier but with a positive outcome:

I think that at first it seemed a bit loud and boisterous when people got together, and as I've gotten to know people better there's been more space for dialogue. . . I'm not sure if that's because I've gotten to know people better and it's simply grown on me or if there really is more space for dialogue. I definitely felt like it was a matter of hanging in there a bit and getting to know people. I also think that it's a different process—I think that a community has its own personality and getting to know individuals is not the same process as getting to know a community, and it's not a process that we get as much practice with as getting to know individuals. I think for me it was a matter of really sort of hanging in there and feeling my way at times. . . just sort of waiting out the honeymoon phase or the awkward phase of trying to figure out what it was all about and what my place would be in it.

Gloria, one of the founding members of the community, has been impressed with how the community supports individuals in their passions:

One thing that I've noticed about UV and have experienced is a willingness to go along with people's visions and ideas and support them. . . and benefit from that and allow people to be priests. For example, early on in the community, I was in my theater arts program. I was learning some techniques in terms of using theater as a tool for building community, exploring things as a community, and I wanted to practice that with UV. So we had one evening session where we did several activities, and [later] we did theater workshops as a community. I know there were people who weren't comfortable with it, but nobody said, "No, you can't do that." In fact they totally went with it. That's just one example. I can think of a lot of other examples of people having a vision for something and the community coming and supporting them in that and that being fairly evenly spread. . . there isn't one or two people who led out in that, like being more priestly than others. Lots of people have had ideas and acted in leadership in those ways.

Heidi, Craig's wife and a participant in the community for many years, raved about how the community "excels in giving practical, functional help." She talked about how her family has received help in areas of housing, food, and financial budgeting. She reminisced about how the community came through with substantial help for her wedding. She added, however, that she does not get the "spiritual input" that she desires and needs for strength to live day to day and that she has to go elsewhere for that.

Bea, another founding member of the community, remembered when Nancy, another member of the community, died of ovarian cancer. The community provided care and support for her in her last months, and then provided housing for family members who came out at the very end. The community designed an elaborate and beautiful memorial service and set up a memorial website. "It was a really big moment where I thought, 'we really are ministering to each other.'"

Charity, a new participant in the community, and a former Marine who disagrees with the community's pacifist stance, talks of experiencing acceptance in the community "no matter where you stand" and commends the ability of members to "sit and listen to newcomers."

Juanita and Wilbert, a founding couple who moved away a few years ago, sent their response by email. They reminisced about the rhythm of common meals and common prayers and how the community became "a haven for individuals who had encountered difficult experiences and needed social, spiritual, and emotional space to find healing and new direction in life."

While most of the reports from members and participants in the community were decidedly positive, some problems were noted. Although Dave is amazed that he never hears gossip or experiences pettiness among community members, another person in a completely separate interview used those very words to describe some less-than-pleasant experiences of the community. Another person maintained that while the community does practice an overall egalitarian and open ethos, sometimes certain members' wishes have been honored over others and that there have been some unhealthy dynamics of favoritism.

Another member of the community has experienced the community "disintegrating" recently and feels that the community does not "strive toward a common goal and is just trying to survive."

Joe talked about all the support he and his wife, Glory, received when their son, Jude, was born but laments that the community is "crippled by the need for money. . . we spend the best hours of our lives at work." Joe wonders how much better community life and outreach could be if people did not have to be away from their homes as much for the sake of employment.

Outward

Despite the long list of former and current outreaches (community members facilitate a neighborhood food distribution, volunteer in a homeless shelter and a school, and organize the local Palm Sunday Peace Parade), community members report a mixed experience with ministry beyond the community. The main complaint seems to be that even if members are often involved in a variety of ministries to the world, they don't do it all together in a way that makes it feel like the community is doing ministry as the community.

Thea, another founding member of the community, puts it this way:

> When Urban Village started, that was one of our questions: would we have a defined ministry? And we ended up deciding that we wanted to focus on community first and let the ministry come out naturally from [our common life]. So I think it's a little bit harder thing than. . . for example, different Catholic orders [which] have a more defined ministry. If you're Dominican you're preaching; somehow, you're involved with preaching ministry. Or if you're Jesuit, you're somehow involved with education. And I think that's true of many of the Protestant incarnational ministries or communities as well. Many of them coalesced around a particular idea of ministry. That isn't us! So we did different kinds of things. . . over time, but it hasn't been a consistent effort over the entire span of Urban Village. I don't know if that's good or bad. It's a different approach. In some ways I think it's allowed people to remain within community, more so than if we had a more defined ministry: if that ministry no longer fit somebody, then it would be more likely that somebody would say, "It's not my life anymore" and so they leave. Where if they're a little bit more ambiguous or more flexible on that. . . they are able to stay in and sort of define their own path.

Bob, another founding member of the community finds this outcome to be disappointing:

> At least in the communities that I've been in, most people who are really committed to Christian ministry find a way to make that their job, and they work in the helping professions. My skills have always been in math and engineering and computers and so forth. . . It's the manufacturers and the engineers and the service providers who create the charitable foundations or the taxes that then get paid to the charitable people, so even when I was nineteen I thought I'd rather work on the productive side of the economy than on the ministry side of the economy, but I think that puts me in a minority. What I'm looking for in terms of a ministry organization is different than most

of my friends. So my ideal had always been that a group of people—maybe as big as a small church like Pasadena Mennonite or certainly as big as UV—would just make a decision on what they were going to do together and we'd really build our life around that ministry.

Bert's always saying UV is achieving a lot if you consider that we all have jobs and we all have families and we all have church and then we just do UV with what's left over from all those commitments. I've always had an ideal that a ministry organization, a ministry community, would be central to the lives of a group of people so that it's not just what's left over, and so both PMC and UV have disappointed me in that way.

Bob, like Joe, has recently been considering the financial realities that impinge on community life and outreach:

I have been wondering if it makes sense to live in the L.A. area where the cost of living is so high because I feel like if you're a professional and you can make forty or sixty or eighty thousand dollars a year, that should be enough for four or five people to live on. . . I always thought that it should be possible, but now I'm starting to think it's not possible in L.A. Anne and I have been looking carefully at where we spend money, and we just spend a lot of it. I don't see how we can cut it down by a factor of three which is what we'd need to do to make my vision a reality, whereas I do think it is more possible other places. . . Anne and I are paying about $1,000 for rent and another $1,000 a month for medical insurance. So that really cuts into this forty or sixty thousand.

Others echoed, to a lesser degree, the downside of not having one central outward ministry that the whole community is involved in. Nevertheless, most members expressed being happy about the ministry that they have been able to do.

Anne, Bob's wife, put it this way,

I think that community helps provide support, making it easier for people to put legs and feet to their faith and to minister to people in the wider community because they have the support of a smaller community. I've seen that working out through the food distribution. . . I think that without the community effort to work with the New Sanctuary Movement it would have been far more difficult to minister in that way. . . I think that even though every member of the community hasn't always been involved in every single way, I think it's been a supportive effort that has certainly made it easier in the midst of life's busyness.

Conclusion

As the person compiling these interviews, I was somewhat surprised at the results. I knew about the dissatisfaction due to the lack of a unified, consistent outreach, but I was surprised by the number of glowing, positive statements about the inward life of the community. My own view is that the community has done a great job of outreach, given our decision to be parachurch, but our inward life has been inconsistent.

Everyone comes to community with unique baggage, expectations, and hopes. None of us knew where this journey would take us when we began it twelve years ago; community never is what you expect it to be. Nevertheless, we seek to be priests for each other and the world. Although we might do some things differently, were we given the chance to start over, none of us regrets our decision, and we eagerly press on to be "a royal priesthood, a holy people, belonging to God, that [we] may declare the praises of [The One] who called [us] out of darkness into [God's] wonderful light" (1 Peter 2:9 NIV).

CHAPTER THIRTEEN

LETTING GO OF THE AMERICAN DREAM: Embracing *Gelassenheit*

by Mark Van Steenwyk

Mark Van Steenwyk is cofounder of the Missio Dei intentional community and Mennonite church in Minneapolis, Minnesota. He is also is an editor of the Jesus Radicals *website and producer of* The Iconocast *podcast. Rather than reflecting primarily on this work, however, Mark shares about his changing understanding of Jesus and the call to be a disciple. His perspectives offer an opportunity for reflection on the way the American Dream has infused North American understandings of what it means to follow Jesus.*

Plastic Jesus

Entombed in plastic
My lord speaks
Brought low by thrifty men
His dangerous words forgotten
Divinity branded
His glory exchanged for a bar code
Cosmic Creator constrained
With a tiny ™
The Lion of the Tribe of Judah
Pushed into a cage
The Lamb of God
Sacrificed at the altar of good taste

The voice of the prophet
Silenced for profit
As affluence pours
Not to the poor
But to the affluent
In a sad twist
Jesus sold at the table
Of the money changers

No one hears the cries
From inside his plastic tomb
As onward Christian soldiers
March to war
We dreamed an American Dream
Eyes shut to the Kingdom Vision
Followers of Jesus lost in the city
With Jesus bound and gagged in the trunk
A day in the life of the Church
Of the Empire
I dreamed an American Dream

—Mark Van Steenwyk

In my senior picture, I'm wearing a red-white-and-blue rodeo-style shirt, a cowboy hat, and cowboy boots. And my shirt wasn't the only thing that was patriotic—I was in love with the American Dream. When I was seventeen, I remember openly weeping before a fireworks show, when "I'm Proud to Be an American" was played over the loudspeakers. In many ways, I was a walking stereotype of American patriotism.

But more than being patriotic, I was religious. To me, Christianity and patriotism were intrinsically tied together. At that time in my life, I wasn't sure if I wanted to serve God through ministry, or serve my country through military service and, eventually, a life in politics. My god was the deity on the back of the dollar bill, where it is written "IN GOD WE TRUST."

What happens when a patriot reads the call to turn the other cheek? Or the wealthy hears the call to sell everything and give it to the poor? Or the snob reads the call to give shelter to the "least of these?" One of two things happens—either they enter into a season of honest struggle or they numb their own hearts and find a way to make Jesus safe.

This is not only true for young right-wing fundamentalists. The truth is, even if right-wing fundamentalists disappeared tomorrow, our most difficult challenges would remain.

If we're honest, most of us tend to justify our desires and dreams instead of taking Jesus seriously. If we're going to enjoy the fruits of the Empire[1]—if we're going to pursue the American Dream—then we've got to find a way to shut Jesus up. We don't need lunatic Jesus turning over the tables of the money changers. We don't want reckless Jesus who hangs out with icky people. We avoid the Jesus whose grand ambition led him to a cross rather than to halls of power.

Rather, we need a comfortable Jesus who exists for our fulfillment. *This* Jesus loves us and has a wonderful plan for our lives. And that wonderful plan looks an awful lot like the American Dream: a nice house, college education, a (more or less) happy family, a generous amount of consumer goods, a couple of cars, a pet, and (if we're really good people) church attendance with up to ten percent of our over-abundance donated to charity. This has become our gospel, with surprisingly little variation.

We have domesticated Jesus and his gospel. If Jesus calls us to anything that threatens to disrupt our American Dream, we either shrug it off as "extreme" or perhaps (if we are progressive) idolize those willing to embrace such extremes and support them with our well-wishes and donations.

Waking from the American Dream

In my mid-twenties, I had a crisis of faith. I realized—and it came as quite a shock—that I really didn't love Jesus very much. I realized that I had treated him formulaically; my relationship with him was little more than a transaction. He died so that I could live forever. Everything else seemed optional. I realized that I really didn't enjoy reading the Gospels and that I thought Paul was a lot smarter than Jesus. Ultimately, I realized that either I needed to re-center my thinking and way of life on Christ, or I had to somehow maneuver myself theologically into justifying my marginalizing of Jesus. For some reason that I don't quite understand, I gambled on Jesus.

This wasn't a quick decision. It required months of cognitive-dissonance-fueled depression. It isn't easy to let go of ideology. My entire identity had become infused with a particular way of being Christian. And much of that Christianity had to die, becoming compost for new growth.

During that time, I came back to some conclusions that were rebuked away in my youth. I encountered a Jesus who called us to love our enemies, to live in Jubilee with the poor, to befriend the outcasts, and to name spiritual forces of oppression.

When one starts to take such things seriously, one encounters resistance. Our society isn't built around those things, after all. We are called to love our enemies, but our society kills its enemies. We are called to Jubilee, but ours is a nation of debt. We are called to befriend the outcasts, but ours is a society of alienation and division. We are called to name spiritual forces of oppression, but ours is a civilization that has numbed us expertly with entertainment and material goods.

But the deepest resistance is found within. The Myth of the American Dream has been woven into my soul. Even though I have changed my mind about so many things, my impulses give away my imperial conditioning.

Several years ago, at Missio Dei, the intentional community I'm a part of in Minneapolis, we had a houseguest named "Gabriel." After a season of unemployment he lost his apartment. He was let go from his job because of frequent absences caused, in part, by his battle with AIDS. One night, a number of us were sitting around the dinner table, along with Gabriel. We were scheming about going to a movie. In all the planning, nobody asked Gabriel if he wanted to join us. For that moment, he was invisible to us. Our imperial script urges us to ignore certain people. It didn't cross our minds that this man was our new friend that we should include in our outing.

In all the many and vast ways that I fail to love my neighbor, my enemy, and my God, I am complicit in systems of oppression. I don't need to be a red-white-and-blue wearing patriot to contribute to global militarism. Likewise, as a formally educated, white, American, heterosexual man, I not only benefit from global structures of oppression, I have been conditioned to accept and enjoy these benefits. If I am going to help bring about the liberating reign of God, I need to not only recognize the ways I benefit from these structures, but also resist them. Part of becoming a disciple of Jesus Christ is learning to confront and resist the ways we have been discipled into Empire.

A story is told about a Zen master who one day received a visit from a professor who wanted to learn about Zen. The Zen master poured the professor a cup of tea and kept pouring even after the cup was already overflowing. When the professor noticed, he exclaimed, "The cup is overflowing; you can't pour any more into it!" At this, the master replied, "Like this cup, you are overflowing with your own ideas. How are you to learn Zen if you don't first empty your cup?"

We think we are open to learning the way of Jesus, but our cup is already full. Unfortunately, we don't notice that it is full. Our lives are full to the brim with tales of the American Dream. The stories read to us as children, the toys we played with, the television shows we've watched, the books we've read, the advertisements we've read, the relationships we've had—these things and more have shaped us. And we have become numb to alternative possibilities.

We are falsely comforted and anesthetized to the ways that we are alienated from one another. We have come to accept it as the way things must be. We accept homelessness. We accept violence and war. We accept marginalization. We accept that some have the right to wealth at the expense of others. We accept many injustices—large and small.

Following Jesus in the United States requires emptying our cup of our internalized imperialism. To love our neighbor, we must understand the ways in which we—through intention or not—are contributing to their oppression. And then we must allow the Spirit of God to refill our cup with a better way—a way of love.

Repent! The kingdom of God is near!

The central Anabaptist practice is arguably that of baptism—a rite of repentance. But far from seeing baptism as a once-and-for-all act of repentance, the early Anabaptists understood it as the initiation into a life of self-surrender, of *Gelassenheit*.

Gelassenheit is a word the Anabaptists borrowed from the mystics. It refers to a deep sense of yieldedness to God's will. While the mystics generally understood *Gelassenheit* to be an inner quiet that, it could be argued, resulted in a sort of detachment, the Anabaptist ethical emphasis understood it practically. *Gelassenheit* isn't simply about an individual's interior life, but their relationships with one another.

Gelassenheit is about ridding one's life of all obstacles to love of God and neighbor. As the early Anabaptist Hans Haffner wrote in his devotional tract *Concerning a True Soldier of Christ*: "When we truly realize the love of God we will be ready to give up for love's sake even what God has given us."

This commitment to yieldedness was central to the early Anabaptist understanding of discipleship. Unfortunately, it has largely disappeared from modern Anabaptist awareness. I am convinced that a spirituality of *Gelassenheit* is central to discipleship today. Far from being a pietistic relic of the past, it is a timely necessity.

What we need now, more than ever, is a new spirituality of *Gelassenheit*: One that seeks to remove all the obstacles to our love. One that understands the intrinsic relationship between love of God and love of others. One that will gladly set aside all privilege, wealth, honor—or any gift of God—for love's sake.

The most powerful thing a community can do in our oppressive world is to come to terms with those things within themselves that prevent them from loving their neighbor and their God. If we are committed to this, we should at least start where Jesus did. Jesus' life and message directly confronted religious, economic, and socio-political inequities. Before we can really understand how to be a part of God's project to transform these inequities, we need to commit to lives of repentance.

Often, we understand repentance purely in the negative. This is unfortunate. While repentance certainly has a negative component, it necessarily includes a positive component. We not only repent *from* something; we repent *for* something. We repent *for the kingdom of God is near.*

This is, I believe, the root of repentance. In order to gain the pearl of great price, we have to sell everything we have first. As long as our focus is on what we're giving up, we'll miss the point. To turn toward God, one must turn from Empire. The kingdom of God and the American Dream are essentially incompatible.

The dangers of charity, colonization, and sentimentalism

About five years ago, I was invited to speak to an adult Sunday school class at a Mennonite congregation. At that time, I hadn't visited many Mennonite congregations. I had assumed that all Mennonites still, more or less, embraced a life of simplicity. I was prepared to share my thoughts about resisting Empire, living simply, and practicing hospitality. I assumed I'd be preaching to the choir, but that I might have a few things to say that would encourage, as well as challenge, the group. I was surprised to discover a deeply affluent congregation that was largely uncomfortable with my message. At one point, a man raised his hand and asked, in a moment of honest anxiety, "How can we resist Empire when we ARE the Empire?"

My experience of Mennonites has been that many are still committed to the harder works of justice—challenging wealth at its root. But even more seem largely content with charity. Charity never challenges structures of oppression. In fact, charity allows the wealthy and powerful to stay in their position of domination while feeling justified. After all, they are generous with their "earned" wealth. Meanwhile the dispossessed, poor, and marginalized are kept in their place. So much of what begins as a pursuit for justice becomes mere charity in the end.

But there are worse dangers than simply reinforcing the status quo with our charity. We can, if we don't embrace a life of *Gelassenheit*, make things worse for the "objects" of our charity. We can unintentionally make imperial converts.

If we attempt to bring about social justice and relational transformation without first embracing *Gelassenheit*, we will presumptuously carry our imperialism with us into the margins. When Empire enters the margins, it is usually considered "colonization." If we are going to be agents of God's love, we must be decolonized. This is, painfully, a life-long process. I don't assume that I'll ever be free from subtly colonizing habits and attitudes. And I certainly won't ever entirely escape from the social privileges afforded to me by virtue of my status as an educated white North American male. Nevertheless, out of love for God and neighbor, I need to name these habits, attitudes, and privileges and submit them to God.

What happens when our institutions bring charity and imperial attitudes into the margins? The history of Christianity shows that the recipients of our "help" become imperial converts who internalize oppression—often assuming that their poverty is their own fault and that, if they are going to be liberated, they need to become like those who give them charity.

How much of our work has the goal of turning marginalized folks into middle-class North Americans? For that matter, how much of our own understanding of discipleship has more to do with the American Dream than the reign of God?

If I don't embrace *Gelassenheit* in my relationships, I will be cut off from my brothers and sisters, and, therefore, my God. I will be condescending—assuming charity is enough, when justice is required. Instead of speaking good news, I will sow seeds of oppression that help keep the marginalized in their place. I will make choices that benefit me, at the expense of the poorest among us.

There is a third danger I want to name in our task of living lives of repentance: sentimentalism. What I mean by "sentimentalism" is the idea that someone is justified by their sense of morality. In other words, if we agree with the sentiments that we should pursue justice, then we are on the side of good, even if we don't really do anything. If there is a danger in "doing something" without really attending to our interior lives, then there is also a danger in "doing nothing" while assuming our hearts are changed.

Contemporary Christianity is filled with folks who believe themselves to be in "solidarity" with all sorts of oppressed people but, somehow, haven't really changed their way of life or the nature of their social lives. You don't challenge injustice by donating money or reading a book. You can't combat racism simply by going to a conference. You can't confront sexism by simply changing the pronouns for God in your writing and speaking. All of these things are probably essential steps in the journey. But they aren't the destination. More needs to change than our sentiments.

Naming the obstacles, embracing *Gelassenheit*

Trying to live in the tension of pursuing justice, embracing *Gelassenheit*, while, at the same time, resisting the tendency toward mere charitableness, unintentional colonization, or self-justifying sentimentalism can be exhausting. But it is worth it. If we long for God's reign to come in full and destroy the walls of alienation, we need to take the risk.

About six years ago, I found myself confronted with this risk. I had befriended a man named "Leonard" who had lived much of his adult life on the streets. I had helped him out a bit here and there with food, enjoyed being his friend, and even called him "brother." One day (about a year into our friendship), as I was on my way home, he said "I love you, brother," and then asked about a place to stay. I realized in that moment that I didn't actually believe he was my brother.

At that point, Missio Dei had been dabbling in hospitality. Folks had slept in our guest room, but usually they were fairly risk-free guests. Now, I was being confronted with my own hypocrisy: I was calling a man my brother but was not willing to act toward him as I would a real brother. Our community was presented with a challenge: we can either continue in our sentimental charity or begin moving (although imperfectly) toward something closer to justice. The more we let go of barriers, the greater the opportunity for justice.

But we can't do it all at once. The journey begins and proceeds with a humble awareness of the obstacles that separate us from one another. We must name them honestly, and then seek to yield those obstacles to God.

What prevents you from deep friendships with folks outside your social location? We are rarely divided by open hostility. The things that often keep us apart are the things that most contribute to our comfort. It isn't simply the greedy rich people who are alienated from the poor, but the comfortable middle class as well. It isn't merely the white supremacist who is alienated from people of color, but the cloistered white family as well.

Oppression exists, not because people are evil, but because people want to secure themselves—because they want to be comfortable. A life of repentance—of *Gelassenheit*—is not about feeling guilty and punishing one's self. Rather, it is a way to cut through the abstractions and myths to see things as they are. It is a way of discovering one's deepest connection with God and people.

If we are to learn Jesus' way of love, a way that gives up all those things that divide us, then we need to be willing to risk our American Dream in hopes of inheriting the kingdom of God.

CHAPTER FOURTEEN

WIDENING THE COMMUNION CIRCLE: Environmental Justice in Camden, New Jersey

By Andrea Ferich

With a deep commitment to Camden, New Jersey, a place at the end of the "waste stream," urban farmer Andrea Ferich shares stories of hope. She encourages Christians to consider our interconnectedness—our communion—with creation in its human and non-human forms. Her story describes the pain of exclusion as well as the joy-filled abundance of inclusive welcome.

Mennonite formation

My journey toward the peace church began in a war zone on the other side of the world. Although my last name is German, I am not an ethnic Mennonite. I grew up in the Mennonite church with my family. I attended Locust Grove Mennonite School in Lancaster, Pennsylvania, and walked to church on Sundays.

My father was drafted out of high school in 1965, straight into the armored cavalry in the United States Army. He fought in the American War in Vietnam, and amidst the violence on the land and people, he found peace. As he rode in his armored tank, surrounded by a cavalcade of armed and marching soldiers, my father remembers a group of Buddhist monks that came walking for peace into the small village his brigade was occupying. He saw about a dozen monks wearing only saffron tunics, walking for peace with no food, no weapons, only prayer.

Dad committed himself to finding a group of Christians that carried out their faith commitments in the same way, following Christ in simplicity, peace, and community. It led him to the Mennonite church when he returned to Lancaster. This war brought my family to the Mennonite church and shaped a great journey of justice for me. The Mennonite church taught me to pursue justice. In the purest sense, justice means changing the oppressive systems that are in place to new systems that allow us to fully love each other.

Justice was a central theme for me while attending the Mennonite church. I learned about traditions of nonviolence, how to fiercely love the land, and about the great work of the Mennonite Central Committee. Yet even with these embodied understandings of justice, the hierarchy of the church loved their accomplishments more than seeking equal partnership with those they "helped."

After five years of church attendance we were still being introduced to visiting clergy and outsiders as "the Ferich family from the city that came to know Christ through the urban outreach ministries of the church." We realized we were never going to be full members. The church leadership chose to remember what they "gave" us rather than recognizing our vital contributions to the community. Perhaps this was done to relieve a guilty conscience or make a show of power. For these reasons my family left the Mennonite church.

The church's understanding of justice kept us marginalized in the community. This is a framework of charity and not a framework for true justice. Within the charity framework the "giver" decides which questions are asked and chooses who is empowered. Charity is justice with an ego. When there is a recipient and a giver, this is not justice. Often the giver works to help the cause of the recipient. The recipient is voiceless and disempowered, relying continuously on the giver.

Interdependent communion

In later years, I found a deep sense of justice within many faith traditions. In Hebrew, the words for justice and charity are the same: *tzedakah*. Maimonides Ladder is a Jewish tradition that creates a tiered structure for justice. The highest degree of charity—above which there is no higher—is to strengthen the hand of the poor with an interest-free loan or enter into a business partnership with the poor person. This model highlights the importance of the relationship, not the gift, and is grounded with compassion, to suffer *with*. In becoming equal partners with the poor, we find that our liberation is tied in with theirs.

This form of mutual dependence, or symbiosis, is common throughout the natural world, revealing the goodness of all creation. When I lived in the rainforests of Belize on a study term with Eastern University, near howler monkeys and snakes that could kill you with a single bite, the deep interconnection of systems radically shaped my understanding. Standing in the sanctuary forest, I began to see clearly the communion in all sanctuaries. We are all interconnected, drinking from the same cup.

I had learned in college about outsourcing and globalization, but there in the jungle I saw the effects of the U.S. consumer society on the land. We say with our mouths that the rainforests should be saved, and with that same mouth eat a burger from the steer that grazes where the forest has been razed.

The women of neighboring Guatemala don't make enough in a month to buy a shirt that they sew which is shipped to the United States We have a connection with these people. We share the same world. Some of us may know them. Some of us *are* them. And some of us might wear clothes that they make. Certainly they are our neighbors. To deeply love our neighbors is to know their struggles and joys, to know that what we put into the air or water here is connected to all the air and water within this world. Our communion is more than drinking from a cup—it is a statement of commitment to all who share it. Our communion is how we love each other and our Creator. It is a commitment to our interdependence, our history, and the widening of the circle of solidarity. Sharing communion together means there is no "downstream." What we do to the land and the waterways will eventually affect my neighbor or me. It is our communion with the land, the land that grows the wheat and the grapevines that become our bread and wine. It is our communion with those who tend it. The Communion Cup is the interconnection of the whole world, the Community of all creation, of all that is good and inclusive.

The church seems to fear this type of inclusivity, the depth of communion seen in the natural world. The witch trials, shunning, and the excommunication of prophets such as Pierre Teilhard de Chardin, Matthew Fox, and Meister Eckhart have condemned people who have spoken the revealing wisdom of the earth. The broken systems of the world are the living and dying body of Christ. The earth is bearing the sins of the people of the world— and groaning.

Many of us grew up in churches where our love for the earth had to be carefully watched, because apparently there is a fine line between loving the earth and worshipping it. This fear has perpetuated within our communities a great violence toward the earth and most of our neighbors. We are biblically mandated to love all creation because of its inherent goodness. If we are serious about loving our neighbors, we must also be serious about what we produce, consume, and throw away.

Perhaps if we meet the poor who live beside the landfill where our waste goes, we will throw less away. And maybe as children of God, we can envision a resurrection that transforms problems into resources and become the community of resurrection that we are called to be. Following the waste-stream led me to Camden, New Jersey.

Finding home in Camden

Camden is an Environmental Justice Community, a place that is disproportionately affected by the environmental consequences of a region. In Camden County, everyone sends their trash, sewage, storm-water, and recycling to our neighborhood. The city of Camden shows the true cost of the consumer lifestyle. Seventy percent of the people living within two miles of multiple hazardous waste facilities are people of color. The air is polluted and the land marked by decades of centralized pollution and poverty. Issues of gender, race, class, and pollution are interlocked in the fabric of poverty.

New Jersey is one of the richest states in the United States and Camden is one of the poorest and most violent cities. All of our trash and waste and polluting industries are often centralized in certain neighborhoods where there are a lot of poor people, people of color, single mothers, and prostitution. These areas also usually have little access to healthy food. Camden carries the cross of the

Empire—beaten, fallen, tormented, and condemned. Similar to places like Detroit, Gary, Jacksonville, St. Louis, and Flint, Camden was once a great center of industry. Now these cities collapse under the burdens of outsourcing and concentrated pollutants from dying industry. They show the true consequences of the American Dream. These places are the indicators of the fading U.S. Empire.

The depths of these systemic problems must be matched with an ever-deepening awareness of systemic justice. Justice is our liberation when seamlessly connected to the "other." It is easy to define what environmental injustice is, but how can we envision environmental justice, something that we have not yet attained?

Sustainable development is the discourse that has helped me to seek justice in holistic ways. Sustainability creates jobs that are good for the environment while also improving quality of life in economic, ecological and social realms.

Measuring sustainability can be a great tool for justice as it helps us to better love our neighbors. Archbishop Desmond Tutu said, "I am not interested in picking up crumbs of compassion thrown from the table of someone who considers himself my master. I want the full menu of rights."[1] Currently, I continue to focus on living for justice and community with the people of Camden and all people who send their waste here. I desire a community of people that support this expression and process of love because their sense of liberation is connected with my own, focused on healing together with all creation.

I moved to Camden because I wanted to hear people's stories. I wanted to help create as much healing as possible. I believe my own liberation is tied to the people of Camden.

This commitment to Camden was birthed out of my experience in Belize. While I was there, a few friends and I created a proposal for an intentional Christian community where we would share everything that we owned. We would live simply, sharing meals and possessions with the poor, and live in a place disproportionately affected environmentally by the consequences of the industrial system.

Thus we started the Camden Community House in the context of a recent resurgence of similar communities across the United States. Many of these communities are similar to the Catholic Worker movement, houses of hospitality and war resistance. Many are of Protestant influence, drawing from Anabaptist teachings.

Marginalized by community

Many of these communities, including the Camden Community House, are joined in a larger movement called the Community of Communities or the New Monasticism. The New Monasticism has a set of "Marks" to live by, a certain platform on which to shape decision-making, vision, and conduct within communities. The New Monasticism is defined as a "movement of Jesus followers who are committed to a new way of life in community."

These communities provide support for members to pursue hospitality, peacemaking, and life together. Yet when a group of people gathers together to define a community as those following a set of Marks, what happens to the individuals who do not fit within that same mold but share similar vision? Is there something that is lost when these communities can point to a group of people and say, "They are not in our community?" This dualistic thinking perpetuates a paternalistic aspect in decision-making, and perhaps never quite leaves the spectrum of charity, since the community decides who will be allowed entrance. When communities, or leadership within communities, choose the Marks over relationships with the people who are seeking to enter, exclusion results.

Although the focus of the New Monasticism is the pursuit of justice, it is as guilty as the Catholic Church or any group or individual of being inconsistent. I am reminded of one of my favorite quotes from Dietrich Bonhoeffer, "He who loves community destroys community; he who loves the brethren builds community."[2] Justice and community seek to widen the circle through interdependence.

I have great respect and have learned a lot from people both within these communities and from those who have left New Monastic communities. The pain of leaving or being asked to leave a community is present for far too many of us. Religious institutions can often be groups of people who see themselves as set apart and therefore don't want to include others who may dilute the substance of the community. How does the church define itself without excluding others? Perhaps the concept of being "set apart" actually means a fierce inclusivity in a world full of judges.

While living at Camden Community House, I was increasingly uncomfortable within the homogeneity of the New Monasticism.

I left the community because some voices were valued more than others. I was not free to define my boundaries for healthy monogamous sexuality, and neither were many others who also left various communities within the New Monasticism. Rather than asking only what exclusivity brings the church, perhaps we should be asking what voices our churches and communities have lost. I would like to see the New Monasticism value the commitments of love, whether with a partner of the same or different gender.

Waste stream justice

Even though I am no longer in the Camden Community House, my relationships with the people of that community are important to me. I have found great connection and mutual liberation with the people of Camden, focusing on widening the circle of justice. And even though I no longer have an intentional community from which I seek justice, the love between my neighbors and me builds a community as we transform problems into resources. We work at the creation of justice together. No more table scraps of charity for us!

In our neighborhood there are twenty-eight known contaminated United States Environmental Protection Agency sites. As we continue to transform our problems into resources, we begin to see that we are sitting on a goldmine of justice. With an unemployment level near thirty percent and with four thousand abandoned city-owned lots, the need for justice through sustainable development is a necessity. Imagine if the armies of this nation no longer fought others for their oil, but rather produced it and taught communities to make their own fuel from the waste-stream!

In addition to the holy bread and wine, there is also the holy oil from the earth. This sacramental substance of blessings has also brought decades of occupied violence to people and land. Two thousand years ago, Pliny the Elder wrote that the two greatest curses of civilization were the discovery of silver and gold. Perhaps oil and gas should be added to the list of natural wealth that ends up damaging rather than helping people in many parts of the world.

You see, the first automobiles on the market were made to run on either gasoline or ethanol. However, in the 1920s it wasn't called ethanol, it was called moonshine. Moonshine was made by people who lived close to the land—the farmers and mountain people. Moonshine can be made from anything containing a sugar or a starch. This age-old approach used agricultural by-products destined for the trash and transformed them into a resource. With the flip of a switch, Ford's Model T converted its carburetor from running on gasoline to running on ethanol.

Certainly the oil industry didn't appreciate it when automobile owners could stop at a local farm and fill up at the still. At that time the Standard Oil Company had a near monopoly on gasoline production. When Prohibition came into effect, a hyperbolic switch was flipped in favor of industrial corporate power. Is it a surprise then, that John D. Rockefeller from Standard Oil also funded Prohibition? During Prohibition, moonshine became illegal. Alcohol wasn't just about drinking. Prohibition was also against local fuel production that was central to the local agrarian economy.

Rather than our fuel production supporting local economies, we have been carried down a trajectory toward dependence on foreign oil and hence, endless war. During Prohibition the Rockefellers held a near monopoly on the gasoline industry. Most of the attempts that the United States government has made to revert back to the use of ethanol have involved corn which at best is an inefficient use of energy.

With waste-stream ethanol production, we could use what is now considered waste to wean ourselves away from foreign oil. We fill our landfills with materials that could be a blessing. In the context of human-induced global environmental degradation, this kind of reclamation could shore up collapsing global and local economies. Perhaps creating fuel from the waste-stream has the potential to be one of the greatest acts of justice. It is far less polluting than standard gasoline and makes creative business partners as the dumpster behind the bagel shop becomes the new oil field. This sustainable development is an act of justice.

The aroma of healing

In January 2011, I had the great privilege of returning with my father to Vietnam, the first time he had been back since the war. Before I left Camden for the journey, a young Vietnamese boy, Vincent, who lives in the neighborhood, came to the outdoor bread oven where we cook every Friday. As Vincent stood beside the wood-fired cob oven he took a deep breath of the bread that was baking in the earthen oven. "Mmmmm, it smells like Nam," he said.

The bread that was baking was Vincent's communion with his memories and his homeland. The same bread might be a key to one of the greatest pursuits of justice of our time. Ingredients of the bread that we can't eat—the chaff and the stalks of wheat—may also be the type of job creation and the justice that this land needs. When I stepped off the plane to meet up with my father in Vietnam I took a deep breath and remembered Vincent, "Mmmm, it smells like the bread oven here."

Vincent and I go to the same church in Camden: Sacred Heart Catholic Church. He is receiving his first holy communion this year, 2011. In our community I hope Vincent and all my neighbors will continue to help widen the circle in our pursuit of justice and nonviolence as we find home with each other.

Although I am Catholic now, I am grateful for my formation in the Mennonite church. May we all, Mennonites or Catholics, people of many faith traditions, inclusively welcome all into our churches and homes. Indeed, our liberation and our healing are interconnected. May we break this bread together.

CHAPTER FIFTEEN

THIRDWAY COMMUNITY:
From Megachurch to Mennonite

By Seth McCoy

*Former megachurch youth pastor Seth McCoy chose to be
ordained by Mennonite Church USA and lead a small intentional community. In this chapter, Seth explores the steps
that brought about this shift. Having joined the Mennonite
church more recently, he offers reasons why a younger generation is attracted to Mennonite faith and theology while
challenging Mennonites to be the kind of family that can
embrace new kin.*

It was a sunny spring afternoon. I was sitting under a tree in Des
Moines, Iowa, waiting. In a few minutes I would meet with the
Pastoral Leadership Committee of the Central Plains Mennonite
Conference and share with them my story and desire to be licensed
as a Mennonite pastor. How did I get here? What would I say?

In May 2009, a group of about twenty of us gathered in Tim
and Alisha Gilbert's living room to discern what God was doing
in us and in our neighborhood in St. Paul, Minnesota. Like the
seeds I had just planted in my backyard garden, another seed had
been planted and was growing. Eventually this new plant would
be grafted onto a much larger family tree with deep roots, Mennonite Church USA. This is our birth and adoption story, with lots
in between.

An early call

I knew from a fairly young age that I was called to the ministry. The small Presbyterian Church I grew up in encouraged me in this direction. In my junior and senior years of high school, I was invited to participate in a Preach-A-Thon. A whole service was given to a few members of the youth group to preach mini-sermons. After I gave a sermon, a woman in the church shared a vision she had while I was preaching.

This was a charismatic church, so sharing a vision was not out of the ordinary. She recounted that she saw oil poured on my head, running over my face. She said God had a special calling and anointing for me. At the time, I thought it was a bit weird, yet I have never forgotten her words or the image she described.

Purposeful pastoring

Out of college I became a youth pastor, a vocation I would stick with for fourteen years. I started out at a small Pentecostal church in Albuquerque, New Mexico. I often wondered how I could be so lucky to get paid for work I loved so much! While in Albuquerque, I picked up a book called *The Purpose Driven Church* by Rick Warren. It made sense to me. Why not run the church more like a business, I thought. Business makes sense, and oftentimes at our church, things didn't seem sensible or relevant to the lives of our neighbors.

About that time, a former youth pastor of Jennifer, my spouse, was sensing a call to plant a church in the suburbs of Detroit. This friend, Chris, spoke at our winter camp one year and asked a few of us if we would consider moving to Detroit. Jennifer and I discussed this invitation and recognized we felt called.

To inspire this new venture, Chris took us to a church outside Chicago called Willow Creek. I was amazed. There were twenty thousand people at this church which had every ministry imaginable. Their building was beautiful, modern, and meticulously maintained. They talked about excellence in terms of giving our very best for God. This meant creating services that were produced like television shows. There were production scripts for every service with each element timed to the second. The church leaders said that visitors who don't know Jesus were giving them one hour. They wanted to do their very best during those sixty minutes and so every second counted!

Encountering questions

In Detroit I learned how to be a leader and eventually moved to a church near Chicago that shared Willow Creek's philosophy. My focus was youth and children's ministry. At one point the church asked me to lead a campaign to raise money for children's and youth facilities. These people committed to giving eleven million dollars over three years!

Eric, a former member of my youth group in Detroit, moved close by to finish his degree at Wheaton College. He agreed to intern with our ministry and after graduation became an associate youth pastor at the church. Eric recommended books to me by N. T. Wright, Stanley Hauerwas, Walter Bruggemann, and John Howard Yoder. Through our conversations, I began to realize that I had misunderstood lots of the Bible, and I grew increasingly uneasy with the church's approach to ministry.

The more I built events and ministries that were attractive to students, the more the kids in my youth group seemed exactly the same as their non-church-going peers. The driving force was getting new people to events and services so they could hear about Jesus who could help make their lives better. It was a style of ministry that is known as "attractional." We looked at what the cultural trends were and reshaped our ministries accordingly. At the same time, we had an assumption that the church played a certain role in society as a service organization, helping our neighbors live better lives.

As I read the books recommended by Eric, who now, along with his spouse, Nicky, is a member of Living Water Community Church, a Mennonite Church USA congregation, I realized my church was missing the Sermon on the Mount. They were also missing Jesus' vision for the church to live the kingdom of God here and now. Now, we talked a lot about Jesus, but it was always related to what Jesus could do for you. He could help you fix your finances, raise your kids, get through a divorce, and of course, he could help you get to heaven after you died. The kingdom of

God was something you thought about after you died, not something you sought while on earth. So Jesus' teachings weren't really important. The gospel was only that Jesus died on the cross to forgive your sins.

At the same time, apart from my church, I was meeting folks who did think Jesus meant what he said. I went with a few friends to visit a place called The Simple Way in Philadelphia, Pennsylvania. There I met folks who were serious about community, simplicity, peacemaking, and justice. I was not the same person after that visit. I was being born again. While I was experiencing new birth, my church was skeptical, which led me to end my role there.

A few months later, a church in St. Paul, Minnesota, contacted me about an open position in youth ministry. When I found out the church was made up of five thousand people, I told them I was not interested. Nonetheless, they suggested I read the latest book by their senior pastor, Greg Boyd. When I picked up *The Myth of a Christian Nation,* I flipped right away to the bibliography. There were all the authors I was excited about!

Not long afterward, I met Greg Boyd, Paul Eddy, and Janice Rohling at a café outside O'Hare airport. I couldn't believe what I was hearing! These folks were not put off by my emerging ideas. They were moving in the same direction. We talked a lot about the kingdom of God and raising up students who would be revolutionary in their commitment to peace and reconciliation. A few months later, my family moved to St. Paul to join Woodland Hills Church.

Mega changes

Woodland Hills provided a place for me to grow up in my new faith and become acquainted with folks who would eventually form the core of a new church in a different neighborhood in St. Paul.

Although the theology of Woodland Hills was different, the structure of the church was similar to the other megachurches of which I had been a part. It began as a church plant looking to follow the "seeker sensitive" model in the suburbs. Though their intentions are different today, the megachurches are not well equipped for discipleship and community.

As many folks come with needs, ministries are created and then are staffed by professionals. It is difficult to avoid the idea that these trained professionals are the ministers and average attenders are not. With a large facility to host services, it is difficult to mobilize people in their own neighborhoods and workplaces. The leaders at Woodland Hills are working hard to push against these things, but a large ship turns very slowly.

I am grateful for the time at Woodland Hills and was amazed to be part of a megachurch that had such radical teaching. This was the first time I saw a real commitment to shared leadership and reconciliation.

And the radical teachings sparked something in me and in others. A few young adults felt called to move into a house and develop a shared life together. A married couple Jennifer and I were close to sold their home in the suburbs and moved into our neighborhood. Soon others started another household right next door to the first one. As more couples and families from Woodland Hills moved in, we longed to form a new kind of family together. The leadership team at Woodland Hills and some of the leaders in our community discerned together whether I should continue in my role at Woodland Hills or become a full-time pastor to this new group. Thus ThirdWay was born.

Life at ThirdWay

I'm not describing a unique group of people. Instead, I see this happening in many places, both with other pastors in my neighborhood, and with groups of Christians who are seeking to live intentionally together. People from many different traditions are discovering the witness of the early church and the Sermon on the Mount. These groups may be looking for a home within a denomination.

And so goes the story I shared on that sunny day in Des Moines, Iowa. A few weeks later I was installed as a Mennonite pastor of ThirdWay. As I have shared this story with Mennonites, certain questions come up repeatedly.

Why does ThirdWay want to be part of Mennonite Church USA?

In my mind, that is better answered as two questions: Why are we Mennonite theologically? And why are we choosing to join Mennonite Church USA?

Mennonite theology has been foundational as we center our life together. Seeking peace, community, simplicity, and reconciliation are actions theologically grounded in the Mennonite tradition. As we try to take seriously our citizenship in the kingdom of God, we are inspired by the Mennonite story of resistance in community.

We are also mindful that Mennonite theology was created through the shedding of blood, sweat, and tears. In a consumer society we are tempted to shop for the most attractive theology without embracing the people who have formed it. For these reasons we have chosen to be part of the story of the Mennonite church. Our connections have deepened as we've met brothers and sisters who have told us their stories. And we believe that our newness to the Mennonite church can be helpful as we seek faithfulness to the past while exploring new ways to embody God's story.

When I was five, my birth mother decided she was no longer able to care for my brother and me. After six months in the foster care system, a young couple in Los Angeles chose to adopt us. In a moment we had parents, aunts and uncles, cousins, and grandparents. This is also ThirdWay's experience with the Mennonite church. We have been adopted, not into an idea, but into a family. What a gift!

What has been hard about planting a new faith community?

Three churches have been planted in our neighborhood in the last year, all using "seeker sensitive" models. Honestly, I am a bit jealous. After all, it would not be difficult for ThirdWay to do the same thing. But since most of us have experience with rapidly growing churches, we recognize that the Sunday morning service can easily become the main focus. This still leaves folks feeling lonely and makes discipleship difficult.

At ThirdWay we want to welcome people at a rate that is sustainable. We feel called to be a community that bumps into each other all the time. This means we will have conflicts and the need for reconciliation. We feel called to plant a church that proclaims allegiance to Jesus instead of to the idolatry of this culture. Lots of people don't want to hear much about the idolatry of patriotism, consumerism, individualism, and hedonism. To be honest, we are still trying to pry our fingers off these idols. Although the work is tedious at times, I am excited about planting a church where community is expected.

We live in a society where commitments are short lived. This not only applies to life in general, but also life within the church.

For instance, if I don't like the church I'm a part of, I will simply leave and find another church that suits me. At ThirdWay, though, we want to take the risk of trusting each other while wrestling with the questions that emerge: "Are we really supposed to see each other as a new family? Can I trust that if I sacrifice financially for these people, I will find support when I am in a tight spot?"

As we're wrestling with commitment of trust, we are gaining a new respect for the community in Acts 2. After all, we deeply believe it is not our effort that sustains this community. It is the Spirit of God who brought this into being, and God will continue to care for us.

By far the most difficult thing for us is when people leave. With the writings of Shane Claiborne and others, there is no shortage of young people who are looking for radical community. Sometimes this means they are looking for a community that is radical in its activism for social justice but noncommittal in relationships to one another. When such people come to us and feel the unexpected weight of our shared commitments, they have no interest in staying. This rejection is difficult to bear and hard not to take personally.

What has been joyful about planting a new faith community?
One of the great joys about planting a new community is that we have the freedom to make our dreams a reality. Each week brings new challenges that we get to face together. As a small group there is also freedom to fail, which I believe is important in community building and leadership development.

Most of us are in our twenties and thirties. We have grown up in a society that demands we live life at a fast pace. Facebook, cell phones, and email have broadened our social circles so much that we need to relearn how to be devoted to a group of people. By walking alongside each other through difficult times, we have experienced the kingdom of God among us.

Thinking forward

A good segment of younger folks these days have realized that "progress" can be a myth and that the "American Dream" is less than fulfilling.

The megachurch movement that began about thirty years ago is bearing unappetizing fruit. Clearly, we cannot inhabit the planet the way we have been for the last fifty years. We also cannot allow multinational corporations to shape our lives with their marketing and gadgets. It's sad to say, but when the church began adopting practices of corporations and reduced the gospel to its most marketable size, we lost our mystery, our wonder, and our imagination.

Younger people are turning to faiths like Buddhism that are more mystical and inspiring, or they are turning to agnosticism. Younger Christians are not so different. We are looking for something that captures our imagination, something that is worth living for. We're not content with a magical afterlife. We want to embody the kingdom of God now.

Mennonite theology affirms that we can experience and share the kingdom here and now. The life of the Spirit invites us again into the story of wonder and mystery. We don't have to live as lonely Christians going to a building to listen to music and preaching. We can live together as we were created, in the image of the God who is three and one, the divine community. We can embody heaven on earth as we work at reconciling deep racial and economic injustices. Indeed, we can take the Sermon on the Mount seriously and join the story that God has been telling from the beginning.

And while this is an inspiring vision, it is not simple. After all, we may be tempted to form a new kind of seeker movement. The ideas of peacemaking, community, reconciliation, simplicity, and justice are already gaining popularity. But are we all meaning the same thing? When the world says "community," the meaning is, "I want to be less lonely." When *we* say it, we mean being radically devoted to each other in covenant relationships, which are difficult.

When our society says "peacemaking," they mean the absence of conflict. When we say "peacemaking," we mean *shalom*, the harmony of all creation restored through the life, death, and resurrection of Jesus Christ.

So although the ideas of community, peace, justice, and simplicity are popular, making a radical commitment to the kingdom of God is not. We will have to carry our crosses, die to our old ways of life and thinking, and be born again as children that need to be taught what it is to follow Jesus. We need a family of elders and sisters and brothers who can walk with us. As the Mennonite church adopts and teaches us, like all children, maybe we can teach Mennonites something in the process.

CHAPTER SIXTEEN

LITTLE FLOWERS COMMUNITY:
On Being a Franabaptist

By Jamie Arpin-Ricci

Influenced by evangelicalism, Catholicism, and Anabaptism, Jamie Arpin-Ricci shares about his formation as a cofounder of Little Flowers Community in Winnipeg, Manitoba. What may seem like a strange combination of inspirations has allowed Jamie and those at Little Flowers Community to wrestle with the strengths and weaknesses of multiple Christian traditions. Jamie's narrative challenges Mennonites specifically to think proactively about the changing shape of church in North America.

From Francis to Menno

It is rather interesting to me that I came to the Anabaptist tradition through a Catholic saint who has been dead for nearly eight centuries. The fact that I started out as a fairly typical North American evangelical makes that journey all the more fascinating. And yet, as I look back, I owe a great deal to that poor little holy man from Italy—St. Francis of Assisi. So how did I get here?

In 2001, my wife and I moved to the inner city West End neighborhood of Winnipeg, Manitoba, Canada. Having been a part of Youth With A Mission (YWAM) since I was seventeen years old, we were there to plant a new ministry center for the Mission in that neighborhood. While my experience with YWAM had largely been related to their discipleship and missionary training programs, we felt that in Winnipeg we needed to live life alongside our neighbors. In other words, while we still offered programs and organized ministry training, our primary commitment was to participate in the life of the neighborhood for the purpose of bringing Christ's kingdom.

This turned out to involve far more than we expected. It became very clear that, as outsiders in the community—because of race, socio-economics, brevity of presence, and other factors—we were the weaker members. While the all-too-common expectation in ministry is for the good Christians to serve the needs of the lost and poor, we found ourselves as students of the poor, whose authority on community life humbled us. This shift in posture helped us settle into the many years it took to truly become locals.

During those years of transition, as we were being shaped by our community, I began to search for examples of those who had been transformed by life among the marginalized. Having seen the oft-quoted statement attributed to St. Francis, "Preach the gospel at all times. When necessary use words," I began with him. I expected a quaint story about this saint to provide some imagery for our life and ministry in the West End. Instead I found my life disrupted by an extraordinary extremist who had the audacity to believe that we could actually *do* what Jesus taught us to do. What started as casual research changed the direction of my life and ministry, including taking vows in a Franciscan third order.[1]

Through Francis I began to see the teaching and example of Jesus through a new lens, especially with respect to the Sermon on the Mount (Matthew 5–7).[2] As I studied the life of this thirteenth-century saint, I began to see how Jesus' words figured centrally into the commitments and lifestyle that shaped Francis and the broader Franciscan tradition. It was then that I began to explore other traditions in church history that had embraced this text with the same zeal. And thus I arrived at the doorstep of Anabaptism.

I believe it is no coincidence that at the same time this exploration was taking shape, our ministry was also facing a significant shift. After nearly a decade, we had begun to see genuine community develop in our neighborhood. We entered into each other's lives and homes, shared meals together consistently each week, and encouraged and supported one another. Sometimes someone facing a challenge would ask for prayer. Other times a guitar would appear and people would sing together. Then one day, a few neighbors approached me and said:

"Jamie, I think we are a church. Will you be our pastor?"

While YWAM plants churches around the world, it is fairly uncommon for us to do so in North America. In our context, if we were to move forward in this direction, it would be important for us to partner with an established denomination who shared our convictions. And so Little Flowers Community was born, the unlikely church planting partnership of Youth With A Mission and Mennonite Church Manitoba.

Little Flowers Community, whose very name reflects our Franciscan spirituality, is a small inner-city church. While only two of our members claim any cultural connection to Mennonite roots, over the few years we've been together as a community, Anabaptist core values have been critical in our formation, as has Franciscan spirituality. What has been most intriguing to me is where these two traditions complement each other—both in how they resonate with shared convictions, but also in the counter-balance they provide through their differences. It is a few of these points that I want to explore here.

Christocentricism and the Sermon on the Mount

As I mentioned earlier, the first and most formative parallel for us between the Franciscan tradition and Anabaptism has been the commitment to the teachings of Jesus, most especially the Sermon on the Mount. For some of us, in the churches we grew up in, taking Jesus seriously meant being morally pure, reading and memorizing Scripture, and telling other people about Jesus. The deeper implications of Jesus' words and example were rarely explored.

St. Francis sought to live the truth of Christ, together with his brothers, in tangible and explicit ways. Franciscan friar William J. Short, OFM, describes the saint's defining inspiration:

> In a word, it was Jesus. To express it in such simple terms today may seem banal to us, or pious, or quaint. But for Francis, the discovery of Jesus, "Our Lord Jesus Christ," was the ongoing revelation of his whole life in the twenty years after his conversion. In his early years he discovered Jesus as the one who led him among the lepers, and made their presence "sweet" to him, rather than "bitter." He then

discovered Jesus the preacher of conversion, announcing the
reign of God. Over the years he began to see more clearly
Jesus as the incarnate Son of God at Bethlehem, then as the
Suffering Servant on Calvary; and finally, "the Lord" of all
things, raised up in glory after his death. And in this Lord,
the glorified Son, he also understood the Trinitarian God.[3]

The degree of Francis' Christ-centeredness and his correspond-
ing radical views on and obedience to Jesus' teaching were revolutionary in contrast to the *Christian-in-name-only* expressions
of faith common in his era. It was this radical commitment that
shaped Francis and his followers into the unique community that
has continued to shape Christendom (and post-Christendom).

It is hard to ignore the possibility that this Franciscan communal
experience of Christ-centered living played some role in the development of the Anabaptist Radical Reformation (along with other
monastic movements of the era). Whether it is the martyred Anabaptist and former Franciscan Leonhard Schiemer, or the likelihood of
Menno Simons' own early education in the Franciscan monastery in
Bolsward, some historical and formational links are likely. Regardless of this, there is a clear parallel with the similarly Christ-centered
approach to faith and Scripture in the Anabaptist tradition.

Both traditions intentionally resist the watering-down of faith in
Christendom. Whereas Anabaptism has taken an active separation
from and resistance to Christendom, the Franciscan tradition has
intentionally sought to be agents of change from within Christendom. This difference deserves reflection. While Franciscans have at
times compromised aspects of their Christ-centered convictions in
light of their submission to church hierarchy, their commitment to
remaining faithful to the unity of the body of Christ is admirable.
At Little Flowers, this tension compels us to challenge the broader
church from our vantage point in urban Winnipeg. We seek to do
this by humbly acknowledging the presence of God actively at work
in the whole historic church, as well as confessing our need for their
unique experiences and understandings.

This tension is not always easy to keep while remaining part of
a Mennonite denomination. Even in the largely evangelical organization that is Youth With A Mission, we are viewed with suspicion
by many. Further, by explicitly identifying with a Catholic saint,

some suspect us of legitimizing Roman Catholicism. The fact is, while we have strong reservation about many aspects of Catholicism, we do acknowledge our Catholic sisters and brothers as part of the one Body that is Christ's church.

The spirituality of economics and the vow of poverty

For many people unfamiliar with Anabaptism, the word *Mennonite* inspires images of quaint Amish farmsteads where groups of people share life in simplicity. While these groups represent a number of Anabaptists worldwide, the image is rightfully linked to a genuine conviction found among most Anabaptist expressions. As Stuart Murray sums it up:

> Spirituality and economics are interconnected. In an individualist and consumerist culture and in a world where economic injustice is rife, we are committed to finding ways of living simply, sharing generously, caring for creation, and working for justice.[4]

This contemporary articulation reflects the historic and scriptural convictions of Anabaptism, especially in its formative resistance to the wealth and compromises of Christendom. Again, this conviction was in part formed by those members of the Radical Reformation who carried with them into the movement their earlier monastic vows of poverty. Often these vows were rooted in practiced solidarity with Christ (and through Christ, with the marginalized). Franciscans embraced this vow of poverty more intentionally than most, at times in excess, threatening their own acceptance within the Roman Catholic Church.

Little Flowers Community, while inspired by such commitments, wrestles with the implications of what it means to embrace it meaningfully, yet appropriately in our own context. Both traditions offer powerful critiques of greed, affluence, and materialism, while presenting alternative ways of life that have in common one core conviction: that such life is only possible as a shared practice within community.

Again, the differences in how these traditions understand and practice these values are also very helpful. For example, the charismatic love for life found in St. Francis (and his followers) is a joy all too commonly missing in expressions of Anabaptism. Many young Mennonites tell me they left their tradition in part because of what they saw as a joyless faith. And perhaps this is more a reflection of their ethnic cultures than an inherent part of the Anabaptist tradition. On the flip side, Anabaptists did not embrace the more rigid and absolutist rejection of property and wealth. Such rejection often complicated and limited the Franciscans from meaningful participation in the life of their communities and the mission of Christ among them. That tension has been a healthy one for our community to explore.

Living in an impoverished urban context has taught us an unexpected truth: that the poor and the rich alike are crippled by their desire for wealth. While the poor suffer for their lack and the rich for their excess, the underlying need for a transformed heart is the same. This remains one of the most difficult dynamics for Little Flowers Community. For those of us who have embraced simplicity, we must be mindful that this "voluntary poverty" is just that—voluntary. Such freedom is an expression of privilege.

Mutuality in community

When Clare Offreduccio decided to follow Francis into a life of devotion to Christ and thus became St. Clare of Assisi, her gender prohibited her from living the itinerant lifestyle of the brothers. Therefore, taking her vows from Francis, Clare went on to begin an order for women—the Poor Clares—who shared cloistered life together, offering hospitality and care for those in need. In many ways, Clare and her sisters (the second order of Franciscans) retained the Franciscan ideals far more than did the brothers of the first order.

One outstanding characteristic of the second order was how they made decisions. St. Clare, in her genuine humility, did not believe that she was to give orders from a position of hierarchical authority. Instead the sisters made the decisions together in consensus, a monumental and historical breakthrough for its time. While Francis did not embrace this value so explicitly, he frequently consulted with his brothers and loathed any privilege, no matter how small, that his position gave him over other brothers. This mutuality deeply distinguished the Franciscan tradition from other orders.

The Anabaptist conviction that the primary place for the exploration, implication, and application of God's truth is in the context of the community parallels this value. Both traditions root this mutuality in the absolutely equal place each person has as members of Christ's body, and thus a role and authority to "teach" each other. This is not a rejection of academia (though Francis was very skeptical of higher education). Nor is it a denial of unique giftings (though both traditions are mindful of how easily some giftings are privileged over others in our cultures). Rather it is a reorientation of the primacy of community in our engagement of truth and practice of mission.

As difficult as this is, Little Flowers seeks to embody these convictions in a community with a higher-than-average incidence of mental illness, poverty, and substandard (or nonexistent) formal educational experiences. These dynamics have challenged our tendency to over-intellectualize faith to the point of abstraction. Our reality demands instead a theology expressed in relationship. The Franciscan tradition has, in my opinion, done a better job at maintaining this, while many Anabaptist communities have adapted modes of religious professionalism. While people are uniquely gifted, say, as pastors, we have all too often given greater credibility to academic accreditation and business-models of "pastor-as-CEO" than to the charisms of spirit-gifted individuals functioning in their vocation as equals among others who are differently gifted.

However, the historical and practical foundations of Anabaptism, where community is the central place to interpret Scripture, have been critical to our continued formation as Little Flowers Community. For many of us, the powerful impact of affirming the essential wisdom of each voice has transformed our corporate pursuit of God and God's mission. Hence, this Anabaptist foundation has fostered a dynamic evangelical movement among our neighbors.

Peace and localism

Another dynamic that both the Franciscan and Anabaptist traditions share is their commitment to being people of peace. Francis modeled a self-sacrificial resistance to the violence of his world. The Anabaptist tradition embraces peace as a central tenant of the gospel which has remained an important (if contentious) marker of identity. Individuals in both traditions have maintained this commitment at great personal cost.

In my experience within the Mennonite community, the commitment to peace has largely been focused on broader, international issues, with some notable exceptions. The importance of such socio-political engagement is critical and should not be devalued. Too many Christians are unaware of or unengaged in the realities of our world.

However, Little Flowers Community shares life together in an inner city context often characterized by violence—gang violence, interracial conflicts, domestic violence, and even the occasional abusive violence by the local government. Our convictions regarding peace are largely born out of a context where our lives are impacted by the immediate consequences of such violence every day. In this respect, we have all too often found grassroots peace initiatives within our city virtually nonexistent. Advocacy for such a response among other Mennonite churches has also proven difficult. We often find ourselves pointed in the direction of other "parachurch" organizations who, while incredibly helpful in many ways, are not trained in grassroots peace initiatives.

While Franciscans have been engaged in broad, international peace work as well, they have also maintained a distinct localism, borne out of their solidarity with Christ and the marginalized. Inspired by Franciscans, Dorothy Day presents one of the best examples in the movement she helped to found, the Catholic Worker. "Such would be the essential thrust of all Catholic Worker efforts: an intense, persisting localism, not as a step toward eventual national effort, but itself the ultimate effort. This localism included both spiritual and political work."[5] We have found this commitment to localism in life and ministry, including our peace efforts, to be an essential part of following Christ in our neighborhood.

A commitment to localism in the Mennonite community in our context is essential. While this is inspired by pragmatic needs in our situation, it is also needed for the sake of the wider Mennonite community—to restore an active, grassroots practice of peacemaking in our own city. The Franciscan tradition offers a model of how such practices can be embraced in ways largely consistent with historic Anabaptist belief and practice. This has been a hopeful possibility for us, but one we are only beginning to explore.

Future trajectory

As a locally defined expression, it has been important for Little Flowers to connect with other individuals and communities who share the values we embrace. Interestingly, we have discovered a notable increase of interest in Anabaptism among people with no cultural heritage in the tradition. Like ourselves, seeking to be faithful to Christ apart from the compromises of Christendom, they have found great resonance and wisdom borne in the Anabaptist tradition.

However, many have found it difficult to engage and integrate into existing Mennonite communities. While the reasons are many and complex, two contrasting themes are quite common. First, many Mennonite communities draw significant identity from their history, including both their cultural and linguistic heritage, as well as their experiences as a suffering and persecuted church. Not only does this dynamic make it difficult for non-ethnic Mennonites to participate in established Mennonite communities, but it has also impacted many young adults from within the Mennonite community. Many of these young people identify with their surrounding culture more than with their parents' or grandparents' ethnic identities. There needs to be a way to include the wider diversity of cultures and expressions within the Mennonite world while still honoring the formational histories that gave rise to the tradition in the first place.

The second dynamic is related. In response to the increasing drift of young Mennonites and the failure to sustain aging and diminishing communities, some Mennonite churches have sought to attract more members through adopting expressions of church more "popular" within the evangelical context. This often results in the diminishing, or sometimes abandonment, of the core convictions of Anabaptism. Our experience as a new church community within a Mennonite denomination has allowed us to see both dynamics at work.

From my perspective as a pastor of a small, inner city Mennonite church, the Anabaptist community is poised to offer a significant gift to the wider body of Christ if we so choose. To offer this gift is my passionate plea. As someone who believes that such an engagement is not only possible, but critical, both for the Mennonite community's future and for the wider body of Christ, may we bear witness to the waiting and watching world around us.

CHAPTER SEVENTEEN

ALTERNA COMMUNITY: Weaving a Tapestry of Reconciliation

By Anton Flores-Maisonet

In this chapter you are invited to travel across the border of privilege to a place where many people suffer for lack of official United States documentation. Anton Flores-Maisonet, a former professor-turned-activist and cofounder of the Alterna community in LaGrange, Georgia, offers glimpses from his faith journey, in part shaped by the Anabaptist tradition. With a commitment to seeking justice for recent immigrants to the United States, Anton's example is an appeal to all Christians to be in solidarity with those marginalized by unjust systems.

> "We reject our country's mistreatment of immigrants, repent of our silence, and commit ourselves to act with and on behalf of our immigrant brothers and sisters, regardless of their legal status."
> —Mennonite Church USA Churchwide Statement on Immigration (2003)

What does it mean to reject the mistreatment of immigrants? To repent of silence? To act with and on behalf of our immigrant brothers and sisters, particularly those who lack legal status?

A local pastor of a small Reformed denomination once shared with me that the "issue" of immigration was threatening to splinter his denomination as its fastest growing churches were immigrant churches. He asked me, "Should illegal immigrants be allowed as members of American churches?"

I sat there listening to this American-born pastor give his best theological argument as to why the church should refuse "illegals" from joining American congregations. To this pastor, unlawful entry into the United States or overstaying a visa was a violation of a just law and, therefore, was not only a civil infraction of the law but was also an unrepentant sin, and he contended that anyone who was known to be habitually exhibiting a sinful pattern of behavior was ineligible to join the church. He recognized that this was a divisive issue within his denomination but he was certain that, as with many other culture war issues, the church should stand firm on what he viewed as the non-compromising nature of the gospel.

How was it that my views on immigration, faith, community, and reconciliation were so diametrically opposed to this sincere, moral pastor? What had caused us to hold such divergent views and to feel confident that each of us was holding a theologically sound argument?

I owe much of my adult faith formation to Anabaptist theology and mentors actively seeking to live these convictions.

Anabaptists remind me that Christ is the center of our faith. We are now aliens in this land and subjects of a new kingdom. Immigrants remind me that if Christ is the center of my faith then Christ is our guide, or our "Good Coyote," who brings us into a new land against the laws of sin and death. I even think good Anabaptist theology would concur that our baptism is our "river crossing" that makes all of us "wetbacks" in this foreign land.[1]

Anabaptists remind me that community is the center of our life. Undeniably, Anabaptists have also understood that this community must not conform to the fallen aspects of this world, and so they often are on the margins of society. Unauthorized immigrants today are pushed to the margins and driven into the shadows of this nation. Anabaptist theology teaches me that the Christian community has no geographical boundaries and that the call to peace, justice, and service, which are all Anabaptist values, compel me to ensure that the centrality of community extends to our politically and culturally shunned immigrant brothers and sisters.

Anabaptists remind me that reconciliation is the center of our work. The 1995 *Confession of Faith from a Mennonite Perspective* states:

Churches are encouraged to find ways to promote reconciliation and to prepare members for communion. The
believers' covenant with one another includes the pledge
of love for brothers and sisters, of mutual accountability,
of confession and forgiveness of sins, and of the sharing of
material and spiritual resources as there is need.

So how did these Anabaptist core values merge into a life of solidarity with unauthorized immigrants? How did Alterna, the missional community I cofounded, form? How did Alterna become a
community comprised of U.S. citizens and immigrants from Latin
America? How did Alterna develop a ministry of hospitality as a
response to a call to accompany immigrants in crisis and advocate
alongside them?

About ten years ago, unauthorized immigrants met me on my
road to Emmaus and invited me into their home for table fellowship. It was when they took bread, blessed and broke it, and gave it
to me that I saw that my work of reconciliation would be in uniting
the church across borders and a broken immigration system.

In retrospect, I can see Alterna's creation as a tapestry woven
by God, the threads of our lives coming together in a beautiful
work of community and love, but most often during this process
I could only see the back of that tapestry where the pattern is a
jumble of threads.

First thread: relocation

The first thread in this tapestry of faith was our response to the call
to relocate into a multicultural and economically diverse neighborhood. In 1995, my wife, Charlotte, and I decided to purchase a
modest two bedroom home in one of the least desirable neighborhoods of LaGrange, a small southern town located seventy miles
southwest of Atlanta. Here we committed to a life of simplicity
and active engagement with our neighbors. We weren't sure of the
fruit of this decision, but we were confident that God would honor
our decision to remain in a neighborhood that other homeowners
had fled in the exodus called "white flight."

Second thread: loss

This thread is one of dashed hopes, searing pain, stubborn determination, and resilient faith. After being foster-adoptive parents for nearly a year, our lives were devastated when a false allegation resulted in the immediate and irrevocable removal of a toddler whom I will always consider to be my son.

The impotence I felt the moment they took our weeping foster son out of my sobbing wife's arms is an experience I would never wish upon my worst enemy; the months of fruitless appeals to a bureaucracy more interested in protecting itself than a child under its watch was quite telling. At the time, I was a professor of social work, so it was even more perplexing to me to watch this supervisor and case manager disregard basic ethical practices such as minimizing foster care displacement and considering the best interest of the child, and use false allegations against us. We and two other families took our stories to the media, and an award-winning series of articles resulted in the transfer of the unethical state employees. But the children were never returned to our respective families. In fact, our foster son was adopted by the foster mother who was given charge over him the moment he was carved out of our home and family.

This painful experience awakened me to the reality of the structural violence that afflicts the marginalized. Having lived a life of relative privilege as a college-educated, suburban American, all my education in social work did not prepare me for the brutal force of what Walter Wink calls the fallen Domination System.[2]

To this day, I point to this dark period in my life as the single greatest factor that led to my becoming an activist. I also confess that I did not escape this trauma unscathed. The toxicity of being on the receiving end of such injustice left a residue in my heart that years of contemplation and confession still have not completely removed. There is, on occasion, inexplicable anger that wells up within me, sometimes from seemingly minor triggers.

In the years since, I have recognized the need to eliminate my inner violence. I have found that contemplative spiritual disciplines are a way of allowing the Spirit to replace anger with forgiveness and healing. Through this trauma, I also recognized the radical and transformative nature of hospitality as all of this was started by simply welcoming a stranger into our life. Furthermore,

I learned a new meaning of faith—faith is a stubborn resilience that, regardless of all evidence to the contrary and in spite of all consequences, empowers us to live out the demands of the gospel.

Third thread: welcoming the stranger

It was that resilient faith that makes this third thread so significant. Within months of our foster son being removed from our home, we welcomed Jairo, our son adopted through a private adoption agency. Born in the highlands of Guatemala, Jairo spent his first year of life with his biological mother, an unmarried indigenous woman with four children who could not feed her children on the unjust wages she earned as a domestic servant. The second year of Jairo's life was then spent in an orphanage in Guatemala City where he was restored to physical health but was in need of a permanent family. So it was in 2000 that Charlotte and I adopted Jairo, a two-year-old filled with personality and love. Our lives were transformed as we loved a stranger in the most intimate of ways. However, we were also awakened to moral demands that were now placed upon us as adoptive parents of an immigrant child. In response to this, we sought to connect with service opportunities in Guatemala and were introduced to the Latin American Anabaptist Seminary (SEMILLA) in Guatemala City.

Fourth thread: La Primera Iglesia Hispana

As a part of our desire to keep Jairo in contact with other Guatemalans, God began to weave a fourth thread into this tapestry. Living in a small town in Georgia, the only means we knew of building meaningful relationships with Guatemalan immigrants was via a new Spanish-language church, La Primera Iglesia Hispana or First Hispanic Church, which was comprised of recent immigrants. God did use this simple act to help us learn more about our son's culture, but God also used it to develop within us a discomforting knowledge of the sufferings of our immigrant brothers and sisters who had been living in the shadows of LaGrange, unknown even to a bilingual social worker like me. It was here in this small Baptist fellowship that we learned much about the rich culture of these first-wave immigrants, the creative ways they adapted to being in a new land with new norms and a new language, but also how they often suffered under the weight of prejudice and overt acts of institutional and individual discrimination in the workplace, schools, medical facilities, law enforcement, courts, and elsewhere.

Fifth thread: September 11, 2001 and the "War on Terror"

The fifth thread was one that changed us all, September 11. After 9/11 and the beginning of the "War on Terrorism," I was left in a state of spiritual dissonance. Born into a Catholic family and then spiritually nurtured by southern evangelicalism, I was uneasy with what seemed to be the normative reaction to this moment of senseless violence. Local churches of all stripes endorsed a call for revenge; churches lined their lawns with scores of American flags but no additional crosses.

Where was the moral and even prophetic voice? Who but the church could mute the drumbeat of war and the relentless shout for endless retribution? In my corner of the world, this voice was nowhere to be found, and I began to feel marginalized, but I was not yet ready to embrace such a spiritual exile.

With my increasing feelings of isolation I began to wonder if our family should end our experiment in countercultural life in LaGrange and seek out a more likeminded community.

Sixth thread: Anabaptism and New Monasticism

Living in Georgia, I knew very little about Mennonites and was unfamiliar with the term *Anabaptist*. Once, during my undergraduate studies, I visited an Atlanta Mennonite fellowship. As a social work student I was intrigued to read in the newspaper about a pastor who was in favor of gun control and who could even articulate a theological reason for his opposition. I visited the church and was impressed with the diversity of the congregation, especially with a significant number of children of color who were adopted into the families gathered here. At the time, I was looking for a church home and, specifically, wanted an ethnically diverse congregation, but something about the form of worship scared this theologically conservative twenty-one-year-old. I remember thinking the songs felt like "hippie" songs that were devoid of the name of Jesus. That was my earliest interaction with

Mennonites; I was impressed with their ability to articulate a holistic gospel concerned with the issues of our culture, but unprepared for worship that took me beyond the privatized and personalized worship style of my "contemporary" church background.

But in college I was ready to listen to the voices of evangelical Anabaptists like Tony Campolo and Ron Sider. Sider's book *Rich Christians in an Age of Hunger* was one of a handful of books that set my life on a new trajectory. It introduced me to evangelicals who felt that social action was integral to a holistic gospel. However, even though I was reading and listening to Campolo and Sider, I never made the connection that they were influenced by Anabaptism. That wouldn't come until later.

It would not be until the mid-90s and after I was married and living in LaGrange that Charlotte and I would make a day trip to nearby Americus to visit the birthplace of Habitat for Humanity. It was there that we learned that Habitat's spiritual mother was actually this unassuming old farm nestled way in the outskirts of this little town, Koinonia Farm, a place whose history of subverting racial injustice predated the Civil Rights Movement. I was inspired and the community's genealogical tree soon introduced me to other communities. I was drawn to these radical experiments or what Koinonia founder and farmer Clarence Jordan called "demonstration plots" for the kingdom of God. I still didn't fully understand the theology that undergirded these groups' call to be the church, living with intentionality and in community, but we admired the authentic nature and consistent ethics of these communities of people who were turning toward the kingdom of God and away from the American values like racism, violence, and materialism that had long infiltrated much of the syncretic American church.

Shortly thereafter, in 2004, I was drawn to a small gathering of mostly young adults who were launching a movement that would be known as "New Monasticism," a group that seemed comprised mostly of young white evangelicals seeking to merge their Word-based faith with justice-oriented deeds within the context of communities intentionally located on the margins of Empire. I was drawn to their earnest desire to incarnate an alternative reality to the church around us.

With these threads, God was truly weaving a tapestry, but oftentimes the only side I could see of this work of beauty was the back side—all frayed, knotted, and ugly. Unaware of the Mennonite core values, I had forming within me a growing desire to have Christ as the center of my faith, community as the center of my life, and reconciliation as the center of my work, but where would I find the community and what would be the focus of my ministry of reconciliation?

Seventh thread: the Martinez family

The seventh thread would become a portrait of the transformative nature of hospitality. And answering the call to welcome the stranger took the form of the covenantal relationship we now have with the Martinez family, an unauthorized immigrant family from Mexico.

Arturo and Norma Martinez, members of *La Primera Iglesia*, were two of our most devoted students in the English class that Charlotte and I offered to our new church family and friends. As an expression of their gratitude and friendship, the Martinezes invited us to their home to celebrate New Year's Eve 2001. Little did we know that this celebration would also mark the beginning of a new life for us. Their home was an old, dilapidated trailer in a trailer park that was littered with beer cans. Inside we saw the roaches and over time the Martinezes would tell us of the rats. They also told us of the prostitutes that a man from Atlanta would bring to the trailer park and how the women would be forced to solicit their services to the lonely immigrant men in the trailers, men who now also had more disposable income than ever before in their young lives.

Norma talked about the fear she had when left in the trailer by herself while Arturo worked. She was in a foreign land with little to no support and no English. Their eldest son, Arturo Jr., was seven years old at the time and was also struggling with the recent and dramatic changes from life in Mexico City to that of small-town Georgia. In his first year he missed thirty days of school mostly due to fabricated "stomach aches."

We left that New Year's celebration joyful for the many wonderful new things we experienced, such as eating a dozen grapes at midnight to ring in a new year filled with blessings. And then after the midnight cheers and embraces, we sat down for a full meal, including my first taste of delicious Mexican tamales. What a momentous celebration!

But we also left that evening a bit disturbed. How could we allow our friends to live in these conditions, isolated and in fear? This was not a question of politics or even ideologies; this was simply a question of friendship and love for fellow church members who happened to be immigrants. Their decrepit trailer was a burning bush, and the roaches, rats, and beer bottles shared this holy ground.

Later that same year, a home on our street was for sale. I knew what I needed to do, but I didn't know where my actions would take me.

The way in which we financed Jairo's adoption was by securing a home equity loan. We realized that even our small home was building equity and that rather than just watch our equity grow; why not find more ways, like our adoption, to use our relative wealth for more redemptive purposes? If our equity could be used to help us begin our family, we wondered if it could also be used to help the Martinezes live in a healthier neighborhood with us as a closer support system.

Without any blueprint, a proposal was made to Arturo and Norma. We proposed opening a new account. The house had an add-on apartment and rent money from it would subsidize the home equity loan used for the down payment, as well as the mortgage, insurance, and maintenance of the house with the Martinezes paying the remaining balance. No money collected would go to our family's personal account and, furthermore, if they remained in the house for a minimum of three years, and then moved away, for whatever reason, they would be entitled to half the equity of our cooperatively owned house. They agreed to this experiment in interdependent living.

In the fall of 2002, Arturo, Norma, Arturo Jr., and newborn Gabriel became our neighbors, and the bond between us strengthened. As far as the housing goes, to this day the Martinezes still live in the same house as co-owners with us and each month their monthly cooperative fee is approximately $150 less than if the house was rented at market rate.

However, interdependence has not been without its challenges. In 2002, the same year that we purchased the home with the Martinezes, Norma gave birth to their second child, Gabriel. This should have been a moment of great celebration, but the arrival of this beautiful baby boy was also met with a life-altering crisis. During her pregnancy, Norma displayed early signs of kidney problems. But it was during delivery that she experienced complete kidney failure and without ever leaving the hospital would go from the maternity ward to the intensive care unit.

Norma's life would soon hit a crossroads of two politically explosive issues—immigration and healthcare. As an unauthorized immigrant, Norma also lived in the shadows of our society without health insurance. Faced with the need for ongoing dialysis services and, preferably, a kidney transplant, our lives were forged together through this crisis and through our intense love one for another.

Now, nine years later, Norma is still dependent on dialysis for her physical life, and we're still dependent upon one another for our life together.

What was God weaving with these threads? With all my unsettled moments of holy dissatisfaction with the status quo, how gracious God was to me! My gifts and passions were interlaced with an immigrant community who continue to teach me much about the forgiveness and grace my heart needed for healing. The resilient faith of immigrants who migrate away from desperation in search of their God-endowed dignity have taught me that, even in the face of life's challenges, or especially in those moments of dehumanization, love is always the more powerful force.

And so it should come as no surprise that the most significant time I clearly heard the voice of God was through Norma, a medically fragile unauthorized immigrant.

Wallowing in self-pity and privilege, I spent those post-9/11 and post-false allegation years thinking the answer was found in moving away from LaGrange. I could only see the ugly knots on the back of the tapestry, and I wanted to move my threads to a different loom. I longed for a likeminded community, yet, time after time, even with viable offers to relocate to communities and ministries that met my presupposed criteria, God had other plans. Our deep love for the Martinez family kept us from accepting any of the new opportunities. If we could have taken the Martinez family along with us, both of our families may have left long ago. But because of Norma's medical condition and our reliance on the local dialysis center, they could not move, and because of our love for the Martinezes, we chose to stay.

In accepting their situation, I have seen the Martinezes draw upon an inner freedom that humbles me. I lament because I want to move; they mourn because unjust laws have prevented them twice from being with parents on their deathbeds. My privilege is denied, but their rights are denied. And still, they seem to rise above the bitterness and hatred that threatened my soul when we lost our son. So one day when I was expressing my vocational angst and the continual inner struggle about whether to uproot my family, Norma spoke to me with genuine empathy rooted in her understanding of an unfulfilled longing for "home" but also with a prophetic directness that I needed to hear: "Anton, you wonder if God is calling you to move because you sense a call to live in solidarity with Latino immigrants. But why would God call you to move when there are immigrants living here who suffer injustice and have nowhere to turn?"

Norma was right. In my small town there are more than enough injustices and crises that confront immigrants. Even to this day the needs can sometimes feel greater than my ability. But Norma left out one key reason that I finally came to realize. While I was struggling to make a commitment to this place, my heart had already made a commitment to a people. It was then that the plea of Ruth to Naomi became my own declaration to Arturo and Norma: "Do not press me to leave you or to turn back from following you! Where you go, I will go; where you lodge, I will lodge; your people shall be my people, and your God my God" (Ruth 1:16 NRSV).

———————————

And so after thirteen years of living in the same neighborhood and in the same house, I was just beginning to understand what God was asking of me. I did not know what my life might look like after simply walking away from a tenure track faculty position that I had held for seven years, but I knew I needed to walk towards a vocational life that would perhaps be without compensation. I did not know how God would fill my time; in fact, in my letter of resignation to the college I wrote that only one thing was for certain, that this move was a "risk-taking venture of faith."

I am now five years into this Christ-following journey within a reconciled community called Alterna. Presently, our members are from Guatemala, Mexico, and the United States. Together we are devoted to freely offering accompaniment, advocacy, and hospitality to those who are marginalized by our nation's broken immigration system.

We accompany the local immigrant who is in an acute crisis. This crisis usually involves a clash of culture, limited English, and unjust laws or policies. Sometimes we are able to see the crisis resolved in a just manner but many times all we can do is offer Christ-like companionship or true compassion—the suffering with another person.

We advocate for the end of unjust policies and laws and for the beginning of redemptive relationships. Advocacy at Alterna may mean helping a local immigrant seek out earned but unpaid wages or worker's compensation benefits. At the state level, Alterna has become a lead organizer seeking to mobilize the church to call specifically for comprehensive immigration reform and for the end of inhumane immigration detention centers and anti-immigrant legislation. We organize and participate in vigils and protests, work with human rights campaigns, and, when necessary, some of us have willingly been arrested for acts of civil disobedience. Advocacy has taught us that if we are to speak the truth in love, we must simultaneously seek to embody an alternative vision to the polarization that presently typifies the "issue" of immigration. Hence, our name, Alterna, comes from Walter Brueggemann's thesis of his book, *The Prophetic Imagination*, which states: "The task of prophetic ministry is to nurture, nourish, and evoke a consciousness and perception *alterna*tive to the consciousness and perception of the dominant culture around us" [emphasis added].

At Alterna we seek to "nurture, nourish, and evoke" by first modeling an alternative reality where U.S. citizens live reconciled relationships, or what Martin Luther King Jr. envisioned as the Beloved Community. Together, we gather for times of shared meals, study, and prayer. Together we welcome guests and visitors into our homes and lives. Together we share our story of physical and spiritual migration with church and community groups. At times we argue, we grow weary, we wrestle with the ethical dilemmas, and we can become disillusioned. But when we find ourselves sinking into despair, we find the strength to love one another, serve one another, and celebrate one another.

This is the tapestry of our common vocation. Christ is indeed the center of our faith. This community called Alterna is the center of our lives. Reconciling U.S. citizens and immigrants is the center of our work. I only ask that Christ be our Good Coyote, leading us into his kingdom.

CHAPTER EIGHTEEN

RACE AND COMMUNITY:
Anthropological Reflections

by Calenthia Dowdy

Anthropologist and college professor Calenthia Dowdy offers perspectives on why many young people of color are not as interested in Christian intentional community as their white counterparts. Her observations speak clearly as to how the American Dream has overridden the gospel message for many Christians. In seeking to embody God-given diversity in community, Calenthia challenges readers to consider the sacrifices that must be made by all.

The question

There it was again, "Why would people choose to all live together and share their money?" The student was sincere in his questioning, but it was a repeat of similar questions I had heard from former students in former classes. Each year I began noticing that the students most perplexed during the discussion of intentional community living were students of color.

This time it was Derek, a nineteen-year-old African American male, who followed up his question with, "When I get married, it's just going to be me and my wife and our kids. We're not living with anybody else or sharing our money." The course I was teaching, "Ministry and the Small Group Process," focused on the formation and function of small groups in church life. The central theme of the class was discipleship in small groups with an understanding that the church is most effective when believers regularly meet together with the triple task of building relationships, learning to love one another, and holding one another accountable. And in this course I always include a mini-lecture on intentional Christian communities.

Most students are aware of The Simple Way in Philadelphia since it was started by a group of Eastern University graduates. Some have read Shane Claiborne's *The Irresistible Revolution*. In my mini-lecture I also include some older, well-established communities like Jesus People USA and Reba Place Fellowship, both in the Chicago area, as well as Church of the Sojourners in San Francisco. I pull up their Web pages showing happy-looking community members, the buildings they live in, and highlights of their mission and vision statements. But, after all this input, Derek just squished up his face, hunched his shoulders, and said "What's the point?"

And what is the point? As a Christian I suppose I could have reiterated all the theological claims I'd already shared in class: That we are not created to be solitary beings; that God desires relationship and so created people; that humans grow and realize their purpose in relationship with God and others. I could have reminded Derek that the early church in Acts 2:42-47 offered a model for believers today. Like them, we are to eat and pray together, sell our possessions, and share what we have with one another. I could have said again that community living is a safe space where believers live out their understanding of who they are in relationship to God, to one another, and to the world. Furthermore, Christians are to be countercultural, energetic participants in God's global activity because of what God had done for us. We are to order our lives in ways that embody the mission of Christ in the world, our neighborhoods, workplaces, and homes. As a part of the Mennonite tradition, with its commitment to nonviolence, I could have included that living in intentional community is one way to be a peacemaker.

There were many theological ways to get at Derek's question. But then I began thinking about what the point was from a very human perspective, via the vantage point of my training as an anthropologist. Why did this question seem most often to come from students of color? Not always, but usually. Were there cultural explanations for the appeal or distaste of intentional community living?

An anthropological lens

Like theology, anthropology tells us that humans are social beings who require the help of other humans to learn what it means to be human. We are born helpless and dependent into kin groups who through the process of enculturation teach us everything we need to know for basic survival. Early humans did not live independent of extended kin in nuclear families. They didn't even live in one place. They were nomadic hunter-gatherers who roamed the land, based on the location of the best water holes, animal food populations, and in-season fruits, seeds, and berries. They were bands and tribes of extended families, fifteen to twenty people who traveled together and whose economic system consisted of subsistence sharing.

In other words, early humans were mobile, intentional, living communities who shared everything they possessed. And they made use of everything they found. Their primary objective was not to store up goods for the future; instead, they used everything they had in the present. Hunter-gatherers were communal in scope, looking out for the collective whole. They shared and practiced reciprocity with other bands or tribes. There was no concept of personal ownership, property, or individual rights. They were consumers, minimal producers, living off the land and replenishing it since the environment dictated everything. These mobile communities usually shunned independence and punished boastful pride and internal competitiveness. They lived as units, not as individuals. Of course, these communities were not without violence and dissention. I offer this history not as a utopian picture but instead to illustrate the origins of human community.

As human populations grew, bands became tribes who became villages who became chiefdoms who became cities and states. Humans learned farming, wandered less, and settled down near water and their crops. They kept animals and built homes. These changes led to storage and surplus which altered everything. Surplus meant security, saving for tomorrow, trading, ownership, and ultimately wealth and independence.

Community and economics

Anthropology shows us that the way people live changes the ways they do economics. Economics impact communities and communities impact economics. Over time, a by-product of a capitalist system based on money is competition and a striving for freedom, cash flow, and independence. In the United States we call it the American Dream and it hinders any notion of communal living. In the biblical story of Saul and his selection as the first human king of Israel, we have a clear explanation of how the twelve tribes transformed from communal life to a nation state with a ruler, class groups, and property ownership (1 Samuel 8). It's explicit in the story that this new system is not God's best plan.

People with little money, resources, or mobility usually rely on one another in substantive ways, sharing what they have with extended family and neighbors. These people groups may have large families and live with extended kin under the same roof. I call this *informal community living*.[1] Proximity is valuable. If in cities, people live in row homes or single dwellings with minimal land around them. People are entrenched in their neighborhoods spending a significant amount of time outdoors, on the porch or stoop talking, laughing and relating to one another. Basic survival depends on the reliability of extended family and neighbors. There is a palpable understanding of how each one is woven into the fabric of family and community around them.

But this usually develops out of raw necessity, not a conscious choice. Resource-challenged people require the nearness of others to co-survive. But poverty and physical survival are not the only reasons humans reside in community. Early Anabaptists chose communal living and radical interdependence. Their faith dictated a different way of living in the world. They were ostracized by mainstream society because of their difference and therefore were even more in need of each other. The American Dream is not compatible with the early Anabaptist's vision of Christian commitment and community. Early Anabaptists made conscious alternative decisions to love their enemies and to allow their children to choose baptism for themselves, rather than baptizing them as infants. These conscious choices put them at odds with church and state leaders, which meant the Anabaptists had to create new communities of support in order to survive.

Cultural anthropology, economics, and human conditioning point to money and abundant resources as the foundation of human independence. Lacking these things, or choosing against these things, necessitates interdependence.

Besides class, another overlapping issue that emerges as part of a complex milieu of understanding intentional community is culture. This takes us back to Derek and the other students of color who don't get as excited about formal intentional community living in the same way as their white peers. Most likely, Derek grew up informally in community.

People of color generally have a great sense of connectedness to family. Frequently marginalized socially and economically, they are there for one another, sharing meals, homes, clothing, and transportation. Community living is not a new idea for most people of color. It is a given.

A family story

My father was raised in a two-parent home with seven siblings in South Carolina. They were the descendants of African slaves who farmed Carolinian soil. By the 1950s and 60s each of the siblings began making their way to Philadelphia where opportunities were said to be plentiful. The unspoken rule was that family looked out for family, at home and in the big city.

By the time my father was sixteen, he made his way to Philadelphia. As each new sibling arrived in Philadelphia from the South, they knew they had a place to stay and food to eat. They were cared for without question until they found work and were able to contribute to the household. At that point, there was the possibility of moving out and getting their own place, but that was optional.

Even as a child growing up in Philadelphia, I remember periods of time when my father's cousin or his niece or nephew would come live with us for a few months until they were able to get on their feet. No one ever went without shelter or meals to sustain them. We were a social and economic support for one another.

In contrast, many white Americans, having had a longer time of access to the American Dream, live in nuclear homes in suburbia with varying degrees of access to resources. But many still express feelings of isolation and lack. White students have told me that they feel as if they missed something growing up, apart from community.

Is it any wonder then that the large majority of people seeking, shaping, and choosing to live in intentional community are white, young, suburban, and middle class? While people of color may take community for granted, or seek to get away from it, middle-class suburban white folks are drawn to the possibilities. Human-kind is simultaneously attracted to community and repulsed by it. We need each other, but we are horribly difficult to live with.

A matter of values

A few important qualifiers: Not all people of color find intentional community living peculiar. Not all white people find it exhilarat-ing. In the past year, I have enjoyed conversations with African American and Latino students who are cautiously reconsidering the concept, the pros and cons, of community living. The idea is less foreign to them than to some students in the past, and many more readily see the biblical basis for intentional community. Nonetheless, racially diverse communities are rare. The variables of culture, class, and ideology make diverse communities particularly challenging.

Aside from committed Anabaptists and other groups who choose to live in alternative ways, the only folks willing to give up on the American Dream are those who have tasted it and called it bitter. Malcolm X called the Dream "a nightmare" because it was designed to benefit majority culture. Non-white people, he said, were not even considered. They were only servants at the table of the dream. Nevertheless, people of color who grow up poor or working class may continue holding on to the hope of "making it" on their own and realizing the Dream, thereby proving their self-worth and their American-ness.

When Derek talked about his future wife and kids living together without anyone else, he was talking about self-reliance and inde-pendence, the values this country taught him from childhood. Real Americans "pull themselves up by their bootstraps" and make it on their own, or so the ideology goes. That same ideology infiltrates theology, church, and every other identity-shaping institution. It insidiously props up the American Dream.

So the Dereks of the world acquire at least three conflicting messages: one, the unstated value of extended family and informal intentional community from which he emerged; two, the need to be self-sufficient as an American because self-reliance is a founda-tional American ideology; and three, if coming from an Anabaptist-Mennonite countercultural position, the value of community and consciously-chosen interdependence. Becoming an Anabaptist committed to intentional community living for Derek might be like "coming home." At the same time, doing this would require sorting through distinct historical, cultural, racial/ethnic, class, and religious baggage. Being black in America and being Mennonite in America are not the same. So the communal table has to be re-set. Are Christian communities fluid enough to change shape when someone new sits down at the table? If intentional communities are to be diverse and inclusive, there has to be willingness to dialogue with others around the table since each new person makes the group a new group. This is not peculiar to intentional living—it is universal to healthy human thriving.

Usually the values and vision of community are set by the founders, or by the majority group who often take their own positions and views for granted. Those may be problematic or they may be non-issues to other ethnic, cultural, or class groups. In most cases, those who do not come from the majority culture of the community will not have the same historical framework, worldview, or appreciation for how and why the community works the way it does. Is there room to broaden the table, and thereby broaden the discussion of life together?

People of color who do find themselves attracted to formal community living are often those who grew up in homes with parents who had the financial resources to live the Dream, yet realized how unfulfilling it was. They learned early on that happiness isn't about excess; it is about becoming fully human through the development of deep relationships.

Sacrificing for new life

As outlined above, these movements are not new; they have been occurring since the dawn of humanity. Economics, or how we give and get "stuff," are a central tenet of living in people groups, whether through subsistence sharing, reciprocity, redistribution, or a market system. Historical framework, culture, values, and ideology shape who will be drawn to intentional living and why. The collective values that dominate a community will reflect who joins that community.

If diversity is desired in community life, sacrifices must be made by all involved. For various people the sacrifices may look different.

For example, some low-income people of color attracted to community may not have the "privilege" of joining community because they are helping support their biological families. The common purse—giving all of one's money to the community—is not a viable option when a significant portion of a person's income is needed by their family. What type of communal sacrifices could be made for this person?

Community already implies sacrifice; diverse community requires even more. Derek, or others entering a community, should not be the only ones to give up something. We all must give up something in order to experience new life. And this new life that comes through change is not a one-time thing. It is our calling as followers of Jesus to embrace an ongoing journey of transformation.

As someone who did not grow up Anabaptist or Mennonite but who entered this tradition as an adult, I have noticed and even appreciated how deeply connected Mennonites are to their historical roots in the European Radical Reformation. For many, this shapes the core of their identity. At the same time, it can leave non-European descended Mennonites feeling left out.

In some ways I can relate, though, as I am also shaped by my African American heritage, grounded in community, resistance, and freedom fighting. But I am frequently forced to ask myself, "Who am I without the trappings of ethnicity, gender, and freedom fighting?" The anthropologist in me suggests that I am no one since I am always bound by time and space, always a black woman. But the Christian says, "No, there is more; there is my spirit who bears witness with other spirits."

Somewhere between flesh and spirit, radically diverse community can happen, even in the here and now. But it requires giving up something of ourselves that is intimate and identity-altering. I am sure our Anabaptist heritage calls us to that. Instinctively, Derek seemed to know this for himself. Can Derek be affirmed for who he is, but also challenged to change? Can we Anabaptist Mennonites be affirmed for who we are and challenged to change as well? As these transformations take place, where will these communities be birthed?

CHAPTER NINETEEN

POETRY AND PROSE:
At Home in Community

By Jesce Walz

Through stories of family, transition and community living, Jesce Walz paints a picture of formation in Christian community. Walk alongside her through the woods of Minnesota and the neighborhoods of Philadelphia as she learns to embrace her story. Listen to what is stirred within you as you are encouraged to consider your own formative stories and experiences.

We lapped through warm water in darkness to where the lake opens wide. The moon shone brightly, highlighting the edges of everything. We held sacred silence as the forest raged: chirping, buzzing, alive.

After some time I broke the spell. I strained to extend my paddle into the moon's reflection, and smacked it through the serene surface. The glowing sphere shattered into thousands of dancing forms. I played with the water, mesmerized by the contrasting light and depths.

A question arose for my companion.
"Where do you see the moon's reflection?"
"What?"

"Reach out your paddle and splash the water where
you see the moon."
She did, and I was transformed as I watched her slap
her paddle down into pure black water.

In the triangulation of her, the moon, and myself, I
knew God's presence. God was in each of us and in
the reaching out from our perches. God was in and
was the moon itself, illuminating everything just
enough to lead us into the night.

Wholly loved, holy dust. We may be strangers or dear
ones. We are one and the same, yet the minutiae of
our differences create an infinite gap between us. Our
lives are made up of intersections; neither of us can
truly know the other's story. Only the Creator dwells
in every mark and moment. I know a God of paradox,
one who holds opposite truths in tension. These tensions form my foundation and lens.

Some strange part of my being will forever inhabit a world that I
knew best when I was very young: The Great North Woods, scrib-
bled in rivers, dappled by cool lakes and towering pines. In this land
my foremothers and forefathers built humble structures, warmed
and fed themselves over fire, sang, struggled, and celebrated.

Bertha Rose Sabourin, the daughter of a saloon owner, was born
in Trois-Rivières, Québec. Her mother passed away when she was
only nine. In her early teens she entered into a cloistered convent of
Poor Clares as a novice. She had not been there very long when her
father, Emile, came to the gate. He stood outside, crying for her to
return home. Eventually she agreed and left with him for another
life outside the cloister.

Bertha was my great-grandmother. She, Emile, and the rest of
the family moved to Wisconsin, where Bertha met George. At eighteen they married, and at nineteen were expecting their first of many
children. They moved to International Falls, a logging boomtown

on the Canadian border. George and his brothers helped to start the Minnesota & Ontario Paper Company. It was 1910.

Marlene was the thirteenth child of George and Bertha's brood, the baby of the family. Bertha held onto the hope that one of her daughters would become a nurse, and because none of the others had done so, Marlene pursued school as she was expected to. Marlene dated and eventually married Gene, a navy man.

A premature birth miracle, my mother came into the world three and a half months early. She weighed less than a pound and could be held in the palm of one hand! Gene was at sea when Marlene went into labor alone; the story goes that he nearly jumped ship when he got the telegram. They named her Lori and baptized her four times before she left the hospital, mostly because they weren't sure whether she'd leave alive.

Lori survived and prevailed. She grew to be a young woman four feet and ten inches tall who loved speech, poetry, classical music, and theater. She was raised in a time and place when women were allowed few paths: mother, nurse, teacher, secretary, waitress, or nun. Defiant, she made a leap to the city in pursuit of education and career. She and my father met in college where they were both studying psychology. They married and returned to International Falls to have me.

———————————

I was born into a world of transition. In some contexts, this word is used to signify lack of stability, life-skills, or commitment. By that definition a person in transition is in need of repair. In my context, transition simply means change, imposed or chosen, and learning to be present as one thing trails off and another begins. To be in transition is to be alive.

Grandpa Gene's parents raised three sons and spent their lives in a tiny white house alongside the brown and curving Rat Root River. As a little girl I dubbed these great-grandparents "Gramma and Grampa Across the Field," because only a field lay between the houses. I ran through it, picking bouquets of buttercups and sweet purple clover. I danced to accordion music or played cards at the kitchen table, sucking on sugar cubes and scratching mosquito bites.

My imagination ran wild like the lush ferns that carpeted the birch groves. I wandered through them in red corduroy and sat on my favorite tree stump for hours. We encountered deer and black bears, went ice fishing, and watched hummingbirds and fireflies from the front porch.

I was the first grandchild in my immediate family. I was spoiled and deeply loved. My parents, grandparents, and great-grandparents delighted in and encouraged me as I learned to sing, draw, and read, so I did these things voraciously. My mother wanted to give her children opportunities that she didn't have; she put me in ballet and piano lessons even when the family could barely afford it. My brother came when I was five and was given the same love, education, and encouragement.

My parents were trying to find themselves then, and were caring for us at the same time. (As I see it now, this process never stops.) They moved our family across Minnesota several times as we grew up. We lived in at least five towns and eleven apartments or houses before I turned fourteen.

In the tumultuous process of settling in, uprooting, and settling again, my brother and I learned adaptability and tenacity. We each reached out and came to trust God as a source of comfort and stability. We were told that we could be anything we wanted, and developed the curiosity and courage to leave an established "home" for someplace new.

We eventually settled in Winona, Minnesota, where I collected a hodge-podge friend group of anarchist punks, Catholics, artists, nerds, and evangelicals. My friends and I dreamed of Christian communes before we knew they existed. I began to travel as soon as I had the permission and resources to do so, and my budding interest in faraway places was fueled. I developed a capacity for creating homes and finding familial friendship wherever I went. At eighteen I left Winona for art school in Minneapolis, carrying with me an anthropological curiosity in culture and a thirst for justice.

We are disconnected from deep roots.
I feel the pain of breaking off from those same roots
That instigated growth, brought fruition, and sent me
    to seed.
I am comforted to remember:
"Very truly, I tell you, unless a grain of wheat falls into
    earth and dies,
It remains just a single grain; but if it dies, it bears
    much fruit."

Launched and grounded.
I am a seed, not a broken stalk.
I carry life within me, and have the capacity to grow
    my own roots and stand.
But I am afraid. How will I grow? Have I fallen in the
    right place?
These worries are not my work.
I wait and wonder.

What if I am an entire field of wheat; what if we are
    an ecosystem?
I can see the patterns we make.
Our lives consist of cycles of birth, growth, death, and rest,
Overlapping in rounds.
These cycles intersect with those in the lives of others.
Our connections propel us through life.

The view is incredible.
I can breathe; I am cut free!
But this moment of comprehension is fleeting and not
    to be sustained.
The ground is still there; I want to breathe and grow
    from it again,
To be present in each connection and departure.
We are seed and cycle, field and forest. Created,
    tumbling, flung.

Let go.

Of course, the forests of my memory are idealized. As my ancestors established home and family, they settled a land previously inhabited by native people. The land was renamed and divided; "the Koochiching" became "International Falls." They built railroads and founded a town employed by one paper mill on each side of the border. They participated in the military, maintained insular family lives, and operated within racist and sexist power structures, questioning anything that didn't fit in.

The mill on the Canadian side of the river still smells like sauerkraut when the wind blows south, but mechanization, technology, and foreign labor mean that fewer workers are needed. The town's population is dwindling. Winds of change are sweeping younger people to larger cities over a hundred miles away.

In stepping out to follow dreams I was raised to pursue, it is apparent that I wouldn't be here if the lives of others hadn't been compromised. So much was invested in my life; so much stolen for it, yet here I am today, just beginning to know myself at twenty-nine.

Like many of my peers, I take for granted the exposure to diversity, education, and options that my grandparents still struggle to understand. I struggle to discern what to take and leave from an overflow of opportunities presented at every moment. I fumble to learn the value of hard work and sacrifice amidst abundance. I resist belief in the promises that progress and efficiency have whispered my whole life. I consider which aspects of tradition to keep and which to throw to the fire.

The juxtaposition of the life I know to the lives of the past several generations fascinates and informs me. These stories illuminate a lived timeline of transition from immigrant culture through industrial, technological, and modern society. Our roots, values, and psychology are deeply connected, but our viewpoints and daily lives differ drastically.

In our global context, an inverse reality exists: We may not understand one another's culture, roots or values, but our daily lives intertwine and tangle as our dependency on resources and labor from faraway lands increases. We are being pulled away from very specific cultures and into a shared culture of globalization.

Today I am a part of a movement that seeks alternatives to this paradigm (of rapid societal expansion and disconnect from local culture and resources). We are rejecting a culture that exploits our world and are building our own culture within its shell.

Amidst this search for a better way, I remember outhouses, well water, digging in the soil, and the smell of a wood stove. I remember relatives who were resourceful, thankful for life, and cared for one another through death.

Many traditions also have shaped my understanding of cultural re-creation. The Anabaptist tradition, with its focus on egalitarian community, simple living, and peacemaking, has been one of these guides. For centuries those who trace their spiritual and ethnic roots to sixteenth century radical reformers have provided examples of what it means to build a new culture within the shell of the old. From their lives we are warned of devastating missteps and inspired by resolute faithfulness. Much of what we call radical is also old-fashioned.

Alongside God we are learning from the past and pushing the boundaries of possibility in the present. We are making a new way, yet this life is something we hoped for long before we could give it a name.

I share the story of my family, part nostalgia and part friction, because it brings me to this place where we intersect. I share it because the transitions and connections that led us to this moment (and lead us to every moment) form me and affirm my faith.

We come from generation after generation of beautiful, flawed children. A story is being told through our breath, life, ashes, and dust. "[Our] days pass away like smoke, and [our] bones burn like a furnace." Our work is to rely on God, rather than our own holiness or what we can build to sustain us. We are truly alive when we walk in trust and gratitude as a part of Creation.

> Roll, collapse into my skin.
> Salty, steady, sun-spoiled.
> Each wave furls into its own reflection
> and fizzles into a thousand foaming fingers,
> Slowly sifting my heart through sand-soiled ankles.
> Dusk casts a veil upon the depths,

Stone-blue, stark against the horizon's empty glowing
   screen.

Stretch and shake me, until I loose the burden I didn't
   know I carried.
Move and break me; I cannot will myself to leave.
Soothe and make me yield within your searching slumber.
And now? You stir me to rise to a still black sky.
Itchy limbs, foggy mind, bleary eyes burning to clarify,
When only silence will suffice.
I submit my beating being to your wonder.

My story is unraveling as I tell it.

I've written to you from rooftops, sidewalks, cafés, fire escapes in Brooklyn, bus stations in Texas, and a trailer park near the Mexican border. But mostly I've been at home: Kensington, Philadelphia, Pennsylvania. I live here with friends in a typical row home on a quieter block of a distressed urban neighborhood.

Today I linger in my room, working on a to-do list, journaling, and organizing details for an upcoming festival of Christian communities. The windows are open to the sound of dozens of children playing with all of their youthful might in the schoolyard behind our house. The woman in charge of recess blows her whistle frantically, trying to rein in their energy. A mail carrier knocks at the door; I chat with neighbors on the front stoop; friends call spontaneously looking for a place to stay the night. I never thought that I could feel so at home here.

It's 3:40 a.m. I am in my kitchen, waiting for granola to finish baking. We're hosting six friends. They rolled in about twenty-four hours ago, and after playing a lovely concert this evening are sleeping in makeshift beds around the house. The granola will be our breakfast.

Tonight is the warmest night we've had in six months. Five houses down, neighbors are barbecuing and listening to music on the slab of concrete that constitutes their backyard. Our house is quiet, but outside, neighbors shout up and down the block, dogs bark, the public transportation goes rumbling by, and a helicopter roams overhead.

I was a little girl eating sugar cubes, talking to my grandparent's "pet" chipmunk, Peanut, in the woods. Now I am a woman with more dreams and disappointments, more uncertainty and opportunity than I can explain. I'm deeply connected to a multinational network of communities, activists, and friends, and am adjusting to living in one of the roughest neighborhoods in the country. I own a house full of guests, things, and a few mice.

I fell in love with the idea of moving to Philly when I was twenty-two, traveling around the country and living in my car. I dragged my feet, though, because I wanted to embrace home, stability, and health in Minneapolis.

Previously I've written about leaving this well-established home in Minnesota for life in Philadelphia by saying something like, "Moving from Minnesota to Philadelphia is the most difficult thing I've ever done," and shared lessons from the perspective of an educated white girl who moved to the ghetto:

> *It's been necessary to practice vulnerability in a strange and sometimes hostile place. Those I've been vulnerable with have loved, challenged, and refined me as we've worn upon and sharpened one another. In many ways, I have more questions and less certainty about how to live out God's kingdom than when I arrived. But the wisdom I desire cannot be gained through correct answers. I wait patiently for wisdom that comes only through experience and perseverance.*
>
> *I've begun the incredibly rich journey of knowing what it is to overcome. I have not overcome poverty or racism; I am allowing experiences and relationships to overcome my own expectations, ideals, and defenses. My spirit has struggled for life, but not been snuffed, and what once seemed oppressive is being lightened by the Spirit of God. I finally feel free to be myself here, and our house has become a home.*

This reflection is from my time in The Simple Way community, a part of the New Monasticism movement, where I lived for my first three years in Philadelphia. As I write this, I realize that the anecdotes and perspective I've given in the past won't do anymore.

Living here has changed me in ways that I am only beginning to understand. I have a deep appreciation for and legitimate critique of the movement I am a part of. Our communities are waxing and waning, and we are collectively overcoming our ideals, struggling and asking serious questions about the future of our life together.

Lately I've been learning about how to live well within a small household in Kensington and have been investing in my congregation, Circle of Hope, connected to the Brethren in Christ denomination. Life with two roommates who are committed to a larger community has been full of work, rest, play, hospitality, and complexity. So was life at The Simple Way, where I lived with as many as nine people in a three-bedroom house, each of us pursuing community with a capital C.

In whatever form it comes, it is of utmost importance to remember that community should not be a machine. In a world focused on the false idols of efficiency and expansion, our work must make room for transition, life, change, death, and the internal movement of God.

We must learn how to extend trust to one another and attempt to live in accountability through relationship, even though we will each fail on some level.

I've given you the story of my community as family because the fruit of my experience exists in intimacy and meaningful relationships that have been built over time. One manifestation of that is the work I do with the PAPA (People Against Poverty and Apathy) Festival. It is a convergence of communities and movements that come together every couple of years. It is inspiring to be with groups of older activists who've struggled and celebrated together for years, as well as younger people like me, who seek a grounded endurance for years to come.

I am learning to be comfortable in my own skin, and to believe that creativity is a contribution of legitimate value. I have thousands of dreams, and manifestations of each of them seem possible.

This hope has come as I've learned to trust and invest. As I dig into life here, friends are seeing both my gifts and my weaknesses and calling them out. I feel more cared for, pursued, known, and invested in than I have in years. The realms of family, friendship, social concern, creativity, and faith are converging cohesively for the first time in my life.

My walk has taken me through labyrinths and endless mountains of switchbacks. I'm still in the thick of it. There is no "there" to arrive at, no particular summit or spanning plateau. I am filled with gladness for today. You are *there*. *Here* is there. We *are* there.

Blooming, open wide
today. It doesn't matter
whether I'm ready.

My heart bursts open like a springtime branch,
Heavy with the weight of its own flowering.
I am overwhelmed, in love with everything;
It's been this way for some time.

We bask in lengthening light,
And bow beneath torrential rain.
The earth stirs, creaks, rumbles.
Creation wipes the crust from its eyes.
Look; it's snowing petals!

We celebrate their colorful death in a flower fight
And brush our cheeks against the branches,
Leaving the morning silent, dewy,
Covered in soft piles of pink and white.
They litter the concrete, concealing trash,
Whispering of crisp green life.

Springtime comes with none of my effort.
It disregards my failure and success.

Maybe this is all I need—
Laughter for no reason that can't be suppressed
That comes when I am broken,
Trying to make things grow within my cracks.
Reminding me—all that I cling to will pass.

I sit on a shoreline throwing stones.
My mind casts into the depths
And reels into my being.

Intricacy within and without, vastness between;
The catch is more than my nets can bear.
Nothing can contain that which is truly alive.
Human beings, human animals.

We jump in and swim through frigid water
Beneath blankets of stars,
Warmed by inner fire,
Comforted by the ebb and flow of friendship and wis-
dom.
What can I give? (Everything. Nothing.)

I am worn and tired.
I move until I can't continue,
And fall asleep in a soft pile of fallen dreams,
To be awakened by rejuvenation and joy
That come from beyond my control.
I want to breathe Your life, in and out.

My hands are open.
If there are goodness and healing for me to carry,
Lend them to me.
Otherwise, help me to be still and near,
To learn what it is to be baptized.
A priestess of creation,
A child at your side.

AFTERWORD

By Joanna Shenk

When I was approached about writing this book, I could think of no better way to tell the story than to have communities speak for themselves. As I traveled around the country, I realized that women and people of color are not often given the opportunity, or choose not to publically share, their stories of community. Creating this anthology felt like a fitting way to deepen already-existing relationships with various communities and individuals, and a good opportunity to get to know some contributors for the first time.

From the start, I wanted this project to give life to the communities and to the individuals writing rather than drain it away. In efforts to keep this front and center, a few individuals had to back out due to other priorities in their lives and communities. During the writing process, others expressed gratitude for the opportunity to reflect and to share untold stories. A few mentioned this project as a catalyst for deepened relationships and continuing writing projects.

From the beginning, I also knew that these stories merely scratch the surface of Anabaptist-inspired discipleship in North America. There are many more communities that have challenging and inspiring stories to share. And the communities and individuals that have shared in these pages could say much more.

This book is an offering of hope to the Mennonite church, to Anabaptist-minded people, and to the broader Christian church. As Vincent Harding said in Chapter 1, it is only when we are in familial relationships that we can wrestle together—that we can "get messy and connected and involved and angry and sorrowful and everything else that deeply engaged people are supposed to get." And, he went on to say, "Love trumps ideology every time."

In my work with Mennonite Church USA, I have been a part of many conversations that question the future of the denomination:

What will it look like? Who will be committed to its ongoing work? What about the people who are leaving? What about the people knocking on the door; will they find a place?

Often I share that I think we have a wealth of resources to engage these questions. As I travel, I meet many younger and older people are who deeply committed to the way of Jesus and to Anabaptist values of community, peacemaking, simplicity, and discomfort with the status quo. Some of their stories are shared here. They embody for us what the future of the church can look like and, indeed, what it already looks like in some ways.

Widening the circle of communion

As Anabaptist-minded people, as followers of Jesus, we have a call to discipleship always before us. This brief volume offers glimpses of how some people have responded to that call. In big and small ways they have chosen to share life together as a response to the individualism and materialism of North American culture and religion.

Through sharing their stories of formation, we are compelled to consider our own formative experiences. For Vincent Harding, his call to peacemaking came while firing a rifle in the U.S. Army. For Hedy Sawadsky, the words of a Palestinian friend still echo: "Go home and work for peace." For Jesce Walz, knowing her family's history of transition enabled her to embrace her own journey.

How do their stories challenge you? What questions do they raise?

As the Mennonite church seeks connection with congregations and communities on the margins of our denomination, how do we relate in mutual ways? Instead of offering charity or "justice with an ego" to those considered poor or marginalized, these stories challenge us to become partners who are accountable.

This accountability, at times, may compel us to evaluate and reimagine the shape of our organizations and communities and congregations. In seeking relationship and input from those who are different from us, we open ourselves to new revelations of God's work in the world. According to Dawn Longenecker, "Sometimes old forms of church and community must die in order for new ones to emerge. If Christians are wise, we will recognize that this needs to happen. We can even help it happen."

Are we willing to ask difficult questions about what is dying and what might be reborn among us?

Often I have been moved by the words of the poet Rainer Maria Rilke. A collection of his poems was given to me as a high school graduation gift, *Rilke's Book of Hours: Love Poems to God*, and this book has been with me since then. Rilke's words have shown up in my sermons, Bible studies, and even occasional songs I have written. Rilke was a wandering writer with a stormy history, and in the midst of it, he repeatedly reached toward God, within himself, and in the world around him. With full recognition of his brokenness, he expected God to meet him.

May we, like Rilke, acknowledge our stories of brokenness, of resurrection, and of hope for what is to come. And may we expand our understandings of what it means to live lives of discipleship, as individuals and as communities.

> I live my life in widening circles
> that reach out across the world.
> I may not complete this last one
> but I give myself to it.

Indeed, the communion circle is widening as we live out the vision that Andrea Ferich and others in this book describe. Let's not be surprised by the experiments of discipleship all around us and let us not be afraid to join them.

"Many Christians are rediscovering living in community, sharing life with the poor, and seeking to love even their enemies," André Gingerich Stoner shared. "Even though we may think of these as uniquely Mennonite concerns, we Mennonites didn't make this stuff up. We shouldn't be surprised that whenever people read the Bible and try to take Jesus seriously they come to this place."

As disciples, let's learn from each other, inspire and challenge each other, "get messy and connected" and walk together in the way of Jesus.

NOTES

Foreword

1. The term "dangerous memory" was articluated by German theologian Johann Baptiste Metz S.J. in developing his political theology.

Introduction

1. Interchurch Relations is a department within the national staff of Mennonite Church USA focusing on relationships with Christians outside of Mennonite Church USA. Currently André Gingerich Stoner is the director for Interchurch Relations and Joanna Shenk is the associate. Together they cultivate relationships with other denominations and Christians interested in connecting with Mennonites. The department was founded on the belief that Mennonites have much to learn from and also to offer other Christians.

2. D. J. Hall, *Thinking the Faith: Christian Theology in a North American Context* (Minneapolis: Augsburg/Fortress, 1989), 195.

Chapter One

1. The phrase *the still in the land* comes from the German phrase *die Stillen im Lande*, which means people who avoid self-display in their living. The first Mennonites in the United States were rural farmers who didn't swear or gamble, who paid their taxes and expected not to be bothered by those outside the Mennonite community. According to Mennonite historian Perry Bush in his book, *Two Kingdoms, Two Loyalties: Mennonite Pacifism in Modern America*, "like good children, they were seen but not heard."

Chapter Two

1. Koinonia Partners is an intentional community, founded in Americus, Georgia, in 1942 by white Southern Baptists Clarence and Florence Jordan and Martin and Mabel England. The community was deeply committed to racial and economic justice and suffered tremendous harassment and violence from whites who saw the Koinonia farm and its members as a threat to traditions of white supremacy. Vincent and I first met Clarence in Chicago where he was speaking at a church, a year before we moved to Atlanta.

2. Staughton and Alice Lynd are activist lawyers and scholars who have worked together in movements for labor justice, peace, and civil rights for more than six decades. Staughton taught at Spelman College and was director of the SNCC Freedom Schools in Mississippi during the summer of 1964.

3. Howard Zinn was a renowned American historian and outspoken social justice activist. From 1956 to 1963, he chaired the department of history and social sciences at Spelman College and became an advisor to SNCC during that time.

4. Andrew and Jean Young were close companions of the Kings and committed community organizers. Andrew served in the leadership cadre of SCLC during the movement and later became mayor of Atlanta, a congressman, and U.S. ambassador to the United Nations. Jean was an internationally recognized educator and advocate for child welfare.

5. Fannie Lou Hamer was a sharecropper, a widely-respected grassroots activist of the Southern Freedom Movement, and an organizer of the Mississippi Freedom Democratic Party.

6. James Bevel and Dorothy Cotton were staff members of SCLC who worked in the area of citizenship education and nonviolence training. Bevel had been a member of the Nashville Student Movement. Cotton directed many of the voter registration campaigns of SCLC.

Chapter Four

1. D. M. P. Freund, *Colored Property: State Policy and White Racial Politics in Suburban America* (Chicago: University of Chicago Press, 2007), 36.

2. Ibid. 14.

3. Ibid. 31.

4. P. J. Paris, *The Social Teaching of the Black Churches* (Philadelphia: Fortress Press, 1985), 14.

5. K. G. Cannon, *Black Womanist Ethics* (Atlanta: Scholars Press, 1988).

6. "Facts, Considerations and Membership of Negroes in the Mennonite Church, 1955," compiled by LeRoy Bechler for the Negro Evangelism Committee, March 1955. Unpublished paper.

7. 1-W was the classification given to conscientious objectors by the Selective Service.

8. C. Eric Lincoln, in the foreword to William R. Jones, *Is God a White Racist?: A Preamble to Black Theology* (Garden City, NY: Anchor Press, 1973), vii-viii.

9. J. D. Graber, "Missions Editorial: The Indigenous Church," *Gospel Herald* (1953): 401.

10. This letter is found in the Mennonite Central Committee Archives Collection, Report Files (IX-12-6), file entitled "Atlanta Mennonite Central Committee, 1961-74" Mennonite Church USA Archives, Goshen, Indiana (MCA-G).

11. Ibid.

12. Ibid.

13. Written Reports, Set #1 by various Urban Pioneers, as collected by Bechler, 2001, found in the "Mennonite Urban Mission Pioneers Interview Project, 2001–02 & Mennonite Urban African American Leaders Interview Project, 2004" (MCA-G).

14. Lee Heights Community Church Constitution and Doctrinal Statement, Cleveland, Ohio, Adopted November 17, 1957.

Chapter Five

1. See: http://www.cpt.org/about/mission

Chapter Six

1. The Confessing Church was created in Germany by Protestant Christians who resisted the government-sponsored effort to combine Nazi ideology with Christianity. Many in the Confessing Church suffered because of this choice.

Chapter Nine

1. R. Sider, "God's People Reconciling" (speech), Mennonite World Conference, Strasbourg, France. (28 July 1984.), http://www.cpt.org/resources/writings/sider

2. K. Kern, *In Harm's Way: A History of Christian Peacemaker Teams* (Cambridge: Lutterworth Press, 2009), 5.

3. D. Friesen and M. Abesamis, *Create Space for Peace: 40 Years of Peacemaking* (Deerfield Beach, FL: TriMark Press, 2010), 81.

4. S. Wiebe-Johnson, personal interview, 20 January 2011.

5. D. Friesen, email message to the author, 11 May 2011.

6. G. Stoltzfus, "History," Christian Peacemaker Teams website, http://www.cpt.org/about/history

7. Friesen, personal email.

8. Ibid.

9. L. H. Nafziger, personal interview, 29 January 2011.

10. Kern, *In Harm's Way,* 233.

11. Ibid., 236.

12. Nafziger, interview.

13. Kern, *In Harm's Way,* 300-301.

14. Nafziger, interview.

15. Kern, *In Harm's Way,* 414.

16. M. Rincón, email message to the author, 15 February 2011.

17. Ibid.

18. M. Rincón, "El Desafio Continua" (speech), trans. C. Rose, Mennonite World Conference, Asunción, Paraguay. (14–19 July 2009.), English translation at http://www.cpt.org/resources/writings/rincon-challenges-continues

Chapter Ten

1. John Howard Yoder, *Christian Attitudes to War, Peace, and Revolution,* edited by Theodore J. Koontz and Andy Alexis-Baker (Grand Rapids, MI: Brazos Press, 2009), 295.

2. John McKnight, *The Careless Society: Community and Its Counterfeits* (New York: Basic Books, 1995), x.

Chapter Thirteen

1. There are various ways of defining "empire." Throughout this essay, I do not use the word "empire" interchangeably with the United States, but rather the larger way of life that is rooted in U.S. American society. Basically, when I write "empire" I mean the social phenomena which create centralized systems of social, economic, and political domination that are reinforced with a shared mythology. In the United States, a fairly serviceable name for that imperial mythology is "the American Dream."

Chapter Fourteen

1. *Today*, NBC TV (9 January 1985).

2. Dietrich Bonhoeffer, *Life Together*. (New York: Harper, 1954).

Chapter Sixteen

1. I am a member of The Company of Jesus, an ecumenical third order in the Anglican rite. It celebrates both Franciscan and Benedictine charisms. http://www.companyofjesus.org

2. For a thorough exploration of our community's engagement of the Sermon on the Mount, see my book *The Cost of Community: Jesus, St. Francis & Life in the Kingdom* (Downers Grove, IL: IVP Books, 2011).

3. W. J. Short, *Poverty and Joy: The Franciscan Tradition* (London: Darton, Longman & Todd, 1999), 31-32.

4. S. Murray, *The Naked Anabaptist: The Bare Essentials of a Radical Faith* (Scottdale, PA: Herald Press, 2010), 118.

5. R. Coles, *Dorothy Day: A Radical Devotion* (Reading, MA: Perseus Books, 1987), 90.

Chapter Seventeen

1. *Coyote* is the slang term given to a human trafficker who smuggles immigrants into a new land against the law. Special thanks to Bob Ekblad and his book, *Reading the Bible with the Damned*, for helping me see the theological view of Jesus as our Good Coyote and baptism as our induction into a life as "wetback" aliens.

2. For more on the Domination System and Wink's theology, read his book, *The Powers that Be* (New York: Doubleday, 1998).

Chapter Eighteen

1. Informal intentional community: the extended family consisting of grandparents and other relatives who live under the same roof out of necessity due to economic lack and support.

ACKNOWLEDGEMENTS

My deep gratitude goes to each of the contributors to this book. Thank you for being willing to share your stories of formation and your "wrestlings" with the church in its many forms. Many of you have hosted me graciously in your homes and communities and have brainstormed with me about the shape of this project. Thank you for your collaboration!

In the Elkhart community I am grateful to the Prairie Wolf Collective—Amyrah, Gaby, Hilary, Jason, Nicole, and Sam—for delving into the complexity of home co-ownership as we renovate and move into two houses together. Thank you for helping me put into practice the values I am so often engaging in my work with discipleship communities.

Thanks also to Rise Up Farms—Adam, Breya, Chris, Corrine, Jeff, Lois, Kenson, Nicole, Shaun, and Simeon—for helping me ground my work in the soil of Elkhart.

To Fellowship of Hope Mennonite Church, for providing a place for me to wrestle with understandings of church, community, and God's work in the world. And specifically to Suella, for your generous listening and thoughtful observations when I have been in the thick of it.

To Mildred Schrock, thank you for warmly helping me host people from many different communities who have passed through Elkhart.

At the Mennonite Church USA offices many thanks go to the Communication team (past and present)—Annette, Chris, Deidre, Johnny, Ken, and Marty—for supporting my work on this book even when it took me away from other projects.

Thanks also to James Krabill for giving helpful advice as a seasoned editor and author.

And to André Gingerich Stoner, I am grateful for your counsel and support throughout the process of this project. Thank you for countless conversations, consistent encouragement, and editorial suggestions as the book came together.

Amy Gingerich and Byron Rempel Burkholder, editors at MennoMedia, thank you for fielding my many questions and providing helpful editorial perspectives.

I am grateful to a number of friends who took part in brainstorming the concept of the book at different points—Nekeisha Alexis-Baker, Caleb Lazaro, Gordon Oyer, Celeste Kennel Shank, Jason Shenk, and Isaac Villegas. Many thanks also to Joshua Kinder, for reading the manuscript and strengthening it with insightful feedback.

And much gratitude to mentors—Phil Bergey, for helping me gain perspective and catch my breath as the manuscript came together, and Elaine Enns and Ched Myers, who connected me with many communities and have supported me in this project with encouragement and counsel from the beginning.

CONTRIBUTING AUTHORS

Vincent Harding is Professor Emeritus of Religion and Social Transformation at the Iliff School of Theology in Denver, Colorado. He is chairperson of the Veterans of Hope Project, which he founded in 1997 with his late wife, Rosemarie Freeney Harding. As long-time activists and teachers, the Hardings began their work in the Mennonite Church in Chicago, Illinois, in the late 1950s and moved to Atlanta, Georgia, in 1961 to join with Martin Luther King Jr. and others in the southern freedom movement. In ensuing years, the Hardings served as scholars, advisors, and encouragers for a wide variety of movements, organizations, and individuals working for compassionate social change in the United States and internationally. Before coming to Iliff, Vincent had taught at Spelman College, Temple University, and the University of Pennsylvania. His essays, articles, and poetry have been published in books, journals, and newspapers. Three of his most recent books are: *Hope and History: Why We Must Share the Story of the Movement; Martin Luther King: The Inconvenient Hero*; and *We Changed the World*, a history of the freedom movement for young people. *There is a River*, his classic history of the early black struggle for freedom in America, has been in print for three decades.

For over forty years, in national and international contexts, **Rosemarie Freeney Harding** was an activist for peace, justice, and racial reconciliation. Beginning in the southern freedom movement in the early 1960s as an associate of the Mennonite Central Committee, Rosemarie worked as an organizer, educator, historian, social worker, and counselor for a wide

Esther Parada

range of religious, community, and educational organizations. In her later years, as she continued to organize and teach, she also maintained a private bodywork and counseling practice that integrated Feldenkrais, Therapeutic Touch, and traditional African American spiritual healing modalities. Rosemarie held a master's degree in women's history, a master's degree in clinical social work, and, with her husband Vincent, was cofounder and cochairperson of the Veterans of Hope Project at the Iliff School of Theology in Denver, Colorado. Rosemarie passed on in 2004. "Mennonite House" is a chapter from her memoir, *Remnants*, cowritten with her daughter, Rachel Elizabeth Harding.

Rachel Elizabeth Harding (*above, left*) is a historian and writer whose work focuses on religions of the Afro-Atlantic diaspora. She holds a PhD in history and an MFA in creative writing, and is author of numerous published essays and a book on Afro-Brazilian religion, *A Refuge in Thunder: Candomblé and Alternative Spaces of Blackness*. Rachel served as a consultant and featured scholar in the PBS series *This Far by Faith*, on African American spiritual traditions. She is also a poet and has published work in *Callaloo, Chelsea, Feminist Studies, The International Review of African American Art, Hambone*, and several anthologies. She teaches in the Ethnic Studies Department at the University of Colorado Denver.

Josh McCallister

Sally Schreiner Youngquist is a current community leader of Reba Place Fellowship, where she has been a covenant member since 1973. She has worked as a high school English teacher, a Mennonite Central Committee administrator, a conference planner, communications manager for the Seminary Consortium for Urban Pastoral Education (SCUPE), and a Mennonite pastor at Reba Place Church and Living Water Community Church. Besides nurturing community, she enjoys reading, walking, and being a grandparent.

Jesse Miller

Celina Varela directs the intern program at Reba Place Fellowship in Evanston, Illinois, and occasionally preaches at Reba Place Church, a member of the Illinois Conference of Mennonite Church USA. She moved to Evanston in 2006 after graduating from Truett Theological Seminary in Waco, Texas. Celina enjoys gardening, singing, and theological discussions with her husband, Peter.

Steve Echols/AMBS

Regina Shands Stoltzfus was born and raised in Cleveland, Ohio, and currently lives in Elkhart, Indiana. She and Art Stoltzfus are the parents of four children: Matthew, Danny, Rachel, and Joshua. Regina has served as an associate pastor at Lee Heights Community Church in Cleveland, and as a campus pastor at Goshen College. She currently teaches at Goshen College in the Peace, Justice, and Conflict Studies and the Bible, Religion, and Philosophy departments. She has a BA in English from Cleveland State University, an MA in Bible from Ashland Theological Seminary, and is currently a doctoral student at Chicago Theological Seminary. Regina is one of the cofounders of Damascus Road, an antiracism education and organizing program.

Tim Nafziger

Hedy Sawadsky lives in the midst of fruit orchards in the picturesque village of Vineland, Ontario. She enjoys hiking and biking, even to the First Mennonite Church, where as a child she first learned the Beatitudes. Half a lifetime ago, while living near Shepherds' Fields in Bethlehem, she began creating petal cards with Holy Land flowers. It's still one of her favorite hobbies.

David Fast

André Gingerich Stoner and his wife, Cathy, have four school-aged children. They live in the Near Northwest Neighborhood of South Bend, Indiana, as intentional neighbors with several other households gathering regularly for meals and prayers and sharing cars, tools, childcare, and daily life. André worked with Mennonite Central Committee from 1984 to 1991 on two peace assignments in West Germany, including relating to U.S. military personnel at a large nuclear weapons base. He served as Pastor of Missions at Kern Road Mennonite Church in South Bend for sixteen years. He presently serves as Director of Holistic Witness and Interchurch Relations for Mennonite Church USA. He is a graduate of Swarthmore College and Associated Mennonite Biblical Seminary.

Marilyn Trout

Since 1979, **Peter and Mary Sprunger-Froese** have been Mennonite peace activists with an ecumenical community in Colorado Springs. They work with homeless people, refugees, and non-violence seekers. They find the Anabaptist story deeply sustaining in their Christianized military setting.

Jim Rice

Dawn Longenecker was born in 1958 into a Mennonite family. She married Jim Rice in 1982 and they have two children, Jessica (age 25) and Adam (age 22). Dawn attends Hyattsville Mennonite Church in Maryland and lives in Mt. Rainier, Maryland. She works with the Church of the Saviour in Washington, D.C., directing their

Discipleship Year Program. She is a member of a Spiritual Support Group focused on dismantling racism and founded by Church of the Saviour.

Tim Nafziger

Tim Nafziger enjoys gathering with people who share values to work and talk together. One such gathering of people is Christian Peacemaker Teams, where he works as Outreach Coordinator. Another is the blog Young Anabaptist Radicals, where he is administrator. He also designs websites, writes, and takes photographs of small and beautiful corners of creation. He lives with his wife, Charletta, beside Lake Michigan in the Rogers Park neighborhood of Chicago, where they attend Living Water Community Church.

Tyler Klassen

Since its founding in 1989, **James Nelson Gingerich** has provided medical care and helped lead the staff at Maple City Health Care Center, a community-based, not-for-profit organization working with neighbors to enhance the health of people in north-central Goshen, Indiana (for more, see www.mchcc .com). This chapter is distilled from a talk James gave in 2008 as Theological Center Guest at Associated Mennonite Biblical Seminary, Elkhart, Indiana; it is available at www.mchcc.com/en/ talk/jamess-seminary-talk-2/. In 2006 he received the Dorothy Richardson award for resident leadership from NeighborWorks America, for his work with the health center. James is a 1980 graduate of Goshen

College, a 1985 graduate of the University of Chicago Pritzker School of Medicine, and a 1988 graduate of the family medicine residency program at St. Francis Hospital, Beech Grove, Indiana. He and his wife, Barbara Nelson Gingerich, are the parents of two young adult sons, Jonathan and Daniel. James is a member of Eighth Street Mennonite Church in Goshen. He enjoys praying with neighbors every weekday morning from *Take Our Moments and Our Days: An Anabaptist Prayer Book*, and sharing a weekly eucharistic meal with friends. His interests include beekeeping, baking bread, weaving, singing from shape-note songbooks, typesetting music, leading congregational singing, and bookbinding.

Mary Klassen

Sarah Thompson is a 2002 graduate of Bethany Christian High School, the Mennonite high school in Goshen, Indiana. Resisting church community pressure to attend a Mennonite college, she chose Spelman College in Atlanta, Georgia, and subsequently got involved in a range of Anabaptist faith-inspired activities (such as eco-feminist anti-war mobilization) while deepening her identification as a U.S. American woman of color. Church involvements include her six years of volunteer work as the North American representative to Mennonite World Conference's Youth and Young Adult Executive Committee and Global Youth Summit Planning Group, as well as service with Mennonite Central Committee and Christian Peacemaker Teams. She returned home to Elkhart to participate in local community organizing and attain a Master of Divinity degree from Associated Mennonite Biblical Seminary, which she completed in 2011.

Jill Shook

Bert Newton is one of the founding members of the Urban Village community in Pasadena, California. By day he works in a public mental health program that houses and stabilizes mentally ill adults who have ended up homeless or in jail. By night he organizes for peace and justice and writes liberationist biblical reflections.

Jared Ingebretson

Mark Van Steenwyk is a cofounder of Missio Dei, a Mennonite intentional community in Minneapolis. Mark is a writer, speaker, and grassroots educator. Mark has traveled around North America, nurturing and networking with radical Christian communities. He is the general editor of JesusRadicals.com and cohost and producer of the Iconocast podcast.

Craig Ferich

Andrea Ferich is the Director of Sustainability at the Center for Environmental Transformation in Camden, New Jersey, where she has lived since 2003. Having grown up Mennonite and now Catholic, she finds great hope within poly-denominationalism. Andrea is an avid writer and filmmaker in Camden, where she lives beside her greenhouse. She makes peace by encouraging sustainable community development and food system security, as well as expressing herself through the arts and loving fiercely. She is the recipient of the U.S. Environmental Protection Agency's Environmental Quality Award and serves as a cochair for the Camden City Food Security Advisory Board and the Waterfront South Network. She enjoys gardening with children and growing imaginations. Visit her blog at aferich.blogspot.com for a free environmental justice garden curriculum and to view her fun and educational garden films.

Rudy Arnold Photography

Seth McCoy was born in Hollywood, California, in the early 70s and is married to Jennifer. They have three children: Judah (16), Glory (11), and Silas (9). He has spent fourteen years in ministry ranging from youth ministry to ministry consultant to church planting in churches ranging from Pentecostal to "seeker sensitive" to Anabaptist. Most recently, Seth has planted a Mennonite church with friends along the University Corridor of St. Paul, Minnesota.

Jamie Arpin-Ricci, is a writer, pastor, and missional church planter living in the inner city of Winnipeg, Manitoba, with his wife, Kim, and adopted Ethiopian son, Micah. Pastor of Little Flowers Community (www.littleflowers.ca), a Franciscan-Anabaptist faith community in Winnipeg's downtown West End, he is also the director of Chiara House (www.chiarahouse.ca), a new intentional Christian community that shares life "on the margins." As a writer, he has contributed to several books and is the author of *The Cost of Community: Jesus, St. Francis & Life in the Kingdom* (IVP Books, 2011) and blogs at www.missional.ca. Jamie is also a third order Franciscan with The Company of Jesus, an ecumenical order under the Anglican rite.

Kim Arpin-Ricci

Anton Flores-Maisonet is the co-founder of Alterna, a Christian missional community based in Georgia and comprised of U.S. citizens and Latin American immigrants. In 2006, Flores-Maisonet left his tenure-track faculty position at a private college to follow a call to a life of solidarity with newcomers from Latin America, especially unauthorized and unwelcomed immigrants. Anton and his wife, Charlotte, have been married since 1994 and have two wonderful sons, Jairo and Eli. Anton is a past chair of the steering committee of Christian Peacemaker Teams. He has also served on the boards of directors of DOOR (a ministry of Mennonite Mission Network) and Jubilee Partners and has taught courses at the Central America Study and Service program (CASAS) of the Latin American Anabaptist Seminary (SEMILLA) in Guatemala.

Jim Toren

Calenthia Dowdy

Calenthia S. Dowdy is a cultural anthropologist who specializes in urban youth culture(s) and Afro-Brazilian life. She teaches youth ministry and cultural anthropology at Eastern University in St. Davids, Pennsylvania. Calenthia was born, raised, and continues to reside in the city of Philadelphia. She's a Philadelphia Mennonite affiliate and has a keen interest in intentional discipleship community living and various expressions of the emerging church movement. Since 2003, Calenthia has been an antiracism trainer with Damascus Road, an antiracism education and organizing program.

Jesce Walz

Jesce Walz is an artist and relational movement-builder. She has been a networker amidst the Christian community movement since 2001. Currently based in Philadelphia, Pennsylvania, Jesce is a member of Circle of Hope (Brethren in Christ) and has been part of The Simple Way. Her creative work includes design, performance art, drawing, writing, event organizing, sculptural installation, and hospitality from her home. She hopes to foster community, creativity, and empowerment as alternatives to structures of oppression. www.Jesce.net

THE EDITOR

David Fast

Joanna Shenk was born in Springfield, Ohio, and raised in an evangelical, charismatic church where her father was the pastor. Although the church, Northridge Christian Fellowship, was a part of the Ohio Conference of the (old) Mennonite Church at the time, most families were not ethnic Mennonites. So Joanna grew up without much awareness of denominational affiliation and identified only as a Christian, not as a Mennonite Christian. As a child, since her father preached pacifism, she thought all Christians were pacifist and did not recognize pacifism as an Anabaptist-Mennonite distinctive. In 1996 her family moved to Dagestan, Russia, to live in the Tabasaran region as Christians sharing the love and grace of Jesus. Joanna and her family were the first Christians and North Americans to live in this mountainous village region. They were met with hospitality, curiosity, and a bit of suspicion. This formative experience opened a new world of cross-cultural understanding and misunderstanding; it also instilled in teenage Joanna the need to believe in Jesus and share the good news of Jesus' message.

Midway through her tenth grade year Joanna returned to the States to finish high school at Bethany Christian Schools, a Mennonite institution, in Goshen, Indiana. This was a jarring shift after the years spent in Dagestan and illustrated to Joanna why she wasn't Mennonite. She felt left out of the close-knit social groups of young adults who had grown up together, and she felt her evangelical faith was not valued or understood by many of her classmates.

Hence, she made up her mind to not go to a Mennonite college and instead enrolled at Huntington University (then College), in Huntington, Indiana. After serving as student body president during her junior year she spent the first semester of her senior year at Focus Leadership Institute at Focus on the Family in Colorado Springs. It was a confusing time for her and she came away with many faith questions.

In her last semester at Huntington she was introduced to the theology of Stanley Hauerwas and John Howard Yoder, in which she found space for her questions. Through encouragement from the few Anabaptist-minded professors at Huntington, she decided to further explore theology and her heritage at Associated Mennonite Biblical Seminary (AMBS) in Elkhart, Indiana.

In 2008 she began her second year of seminary by moving into the Jubilee House (see Chapter 11) in Elkhart. It was a place of love, acceptance, and formation as she wrestled with what it meant to come from her family of origin as a woman and a follower of Jesus. Having found a theological home among Mennonites, she decided to become a member at Fellowship of Hope Mennonite Church. In 2009, she graduated from AMBS with an MA degree in Theological Studies.

Currently Joanna lives in the vibrant neighborhood of south central Elkhart, Indiana, where she is a part of a cohousing community, the Prairie Wolf Collective. She also helped to start Rise Up Farms, a permaculture farming initiative that seeks to connect people in Elkhart with locally grown food. Since 2010, she has been a cohost and coproducer of The Iconocast, a twice-monthly podcast hosted at JesusRadicals.com. Joanna also works with Mennonite Church USA's national staff as associate for interchurch relations and communication. In this role she is a writer, editor, and link between the denomination and other Christians who are interested in community and discipleship stemming from the Anabaptist tradition.